B|ARS MÜNCHEN

ISTVÁN COCRON

B|ARS MÜNCHEN

Bar-Guide

ISTVÁN COCRON

Alle Bars
All Bars

MEATINGRAUM — **12**

TOBI'S KITCHEN — **16**

KATOPAZZO — **20**

NIEDERLASSUNG — **24**

PANTHER — **28**

W XYZ BAR — **32**

ZEPHYR BAR — **36**

DAS PROVISORIUM — **40**

SKYBAR — **44**

FREEBIRD BAR — **48**

OSKAR MARIA BRASSERIE — **52**

SCHUMANN'S TAGESBAR — **56**

VEGA BAR — **60**

SCHUMANN'S — **64**

LEONARDO ROYAL HOTEL — **68**

LE FLORIDA — **72**

HELENE — **76**

MUNICH PALACE HOTEL — **80**

KISTE — **84**

WEDDING CHAPEL — **88**

auf einen
at a

BEN'S BAR — **92**

SALON IRKUTSK — **96**

SCHWARZER ENGEL — **100**

CABARET PIGALLE — **104**

ROBINSON'S BAR — **108**

KAMMERSPIELE BAR — **112**

COHIBAR CITY — **116**

CHAMPAGNE CHARACTERS — **120**

L'APERITIVO — **124**

MUC-BAR — **128**

BENKO BAR — **132**

HOME — **136**

HEILIGGEIST 1 BAR — **140**

BUCCI BAR — **144**

LES FLEURS DU MAL — **148**

KOOKS — **152**

RATTLESNAKE SALOON — **156**

BRUCKMANN'S BAR — **160**

HEART — **164**

COUCH CLUB — **168**

B|ARS MÜNCHEN

Blick!
glance!

DIE REGISTRATUR — **172**

KILOMBO — **176**

JOHANNIS CAFÉ — **180**

CAFÉ CORD — **184**

STADION — **188**

PALAU — **192**

BAR COMERCIAL — **196**

LOLA — **200**

STAMMBAR — **204**

BLUE SPA LOUNGE & TERRASSE — **208**

GREY'S BAR — **212**

GEYERWALLY — **216**

BAR GABÁNYI — **220**

MONOPOL KINO — **224**

RATIONALTHEATER — **228**

HAVANA CLUB — **232**

BAR TABACCO — **236**

GARÇON — **240**

THE HIGH — **244**

BIARS MÜNCHEN

„DIE SEELE EINER GUTEN BAR IST SCHEU –
SIE SCHLÜPFT ERST INS BILD,
WENN SIE NICHT MEHR ABGELENKT IST."
Franz Braun

Vorwort

Freunde der Nacht!

Das zweite Buch aus dem Hause Bars Monaco ist fertig und bereit entdeckt zu werden. Ich freue mich sehr, dass wir es geschafft haben, 59 weitere Bars vorzustellen.

Das vorliegende Buch zeigt wahre Schmuckstücke und lädt Euch ein, nach draußen zu gehen und in das Münchner Nachtleben zu stürzen. Spannende, neue und überraschende Seiten dieser wunderbaren Stadt sind garantiert.

Es versteht sich von selbst, dass sich keine der Bars in das Buch einkaufen konnte. Wir machen keine Werbung, sondern haben einfach nur Spaß daran, nach den Perlen der Stadt zu tauchen.

Über Anmerkungen, Anregungen und weitere Ideen, freut sich

István Cocron

"YEAH!"
anonymous

Intro-
duction

Friends of the night!

The second book by the author of Bars Monaco is finished and ready to be discovered. I am very happy that we have managed to introduce 59 more bars.

This book presents true pieces of jewelry and invites you to go outside and plunge into Munich's nightlife. Exciting, new and surprising sides of this wonderful city areguaranteed.
It goes without saying that none of the bars could buy their way into the book.We do not make any advertising, but just have fun exploring the pearls of the city.

We are always happy with comments, suggestions and other ideas. Yours

István Cocron

Meating-raum

Konzeptküche; Themenabende; Winzer zu Besuch; James Bond-Filme gucken; Lecker Essen und Trinken; Zwei große Tische für Alle; Private Supper Clubs willkommen; Leidenschaftliche Betreiber

Concept kitchen; Theme nights; Winery to visit; Watch James Bond movies; Delicious food and drink; Two large tables for all; Private supper clubs welcomes; Passionate operators

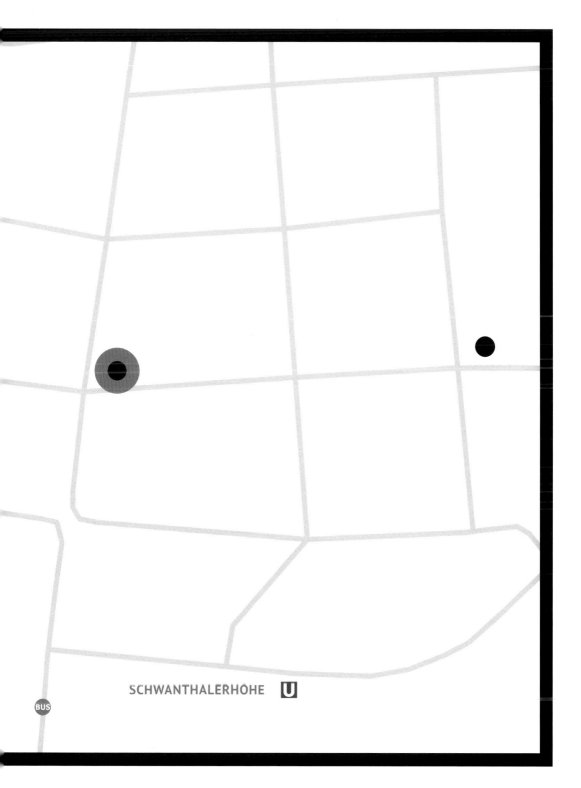

LOCATION Gollierstraße 38, 80339 München • PHONE +49(0)171 993 14 24
WEB meatingraum.de • MAIL eat@meatingraum.de

Tobi's Kitchen

Bar mit Kicker, Backgammon, Looping Louie und vielen anderen Spielen; Kleine Küche; Die Leute sollen sich unterhalten können; Sofaecke mit Nintendoanschluss; Der Chef spielt gerne mit; Hammer Comicsammlung in den Waschräumen

Bar with kicker, backgammon, looping Louie and many other games; Small kitchen; People should be able to talk; Sofa corner with Nintendo connection; The boss likes to play too; Hammer collection of comics in the washroom

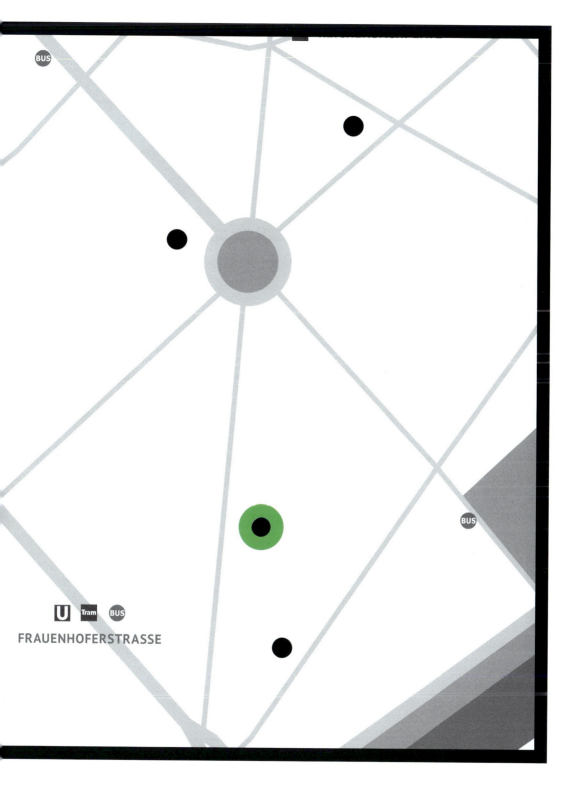

LOCATION Reichenbachstraße 37, 80469 München • **PHONE** +49 (0)89 381 685 501
WEB www.tobiskitchen.de • **MAIL** info@rockbox.de

TOBI'S KITCHEN

Kato-pazzo

Zwei Etagen; Bar und Restaurant; Sehr gemütlich; Gestaltet von zwei Architekten; Bezahlbare Drinks; Gutes Essen

Two floors; Bar and restaurant; Very cozy; Designed by two architects; Affordable drinks; Good food

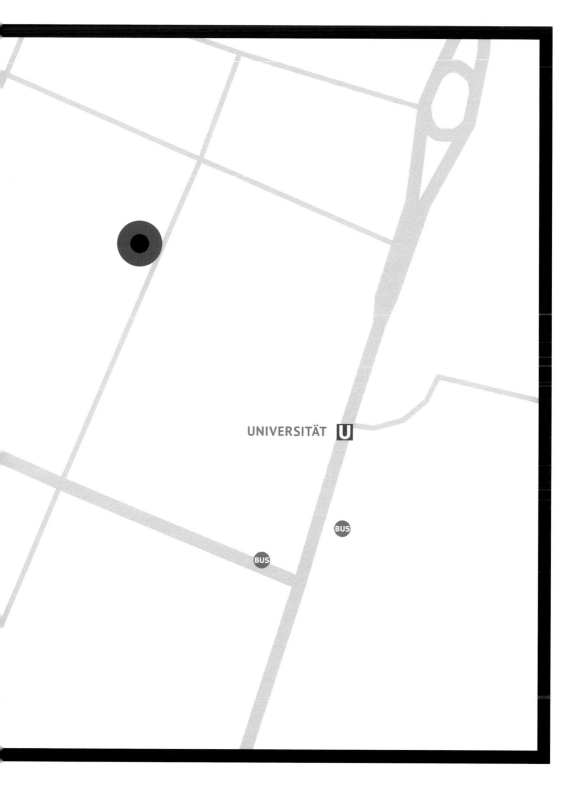

LOCATION Amalienstraße 87, 80799 München • **PHONE** +49 (0)89 443 87 114
WEB www.katopazzo.de • **MAIL** info@katopazzo.de

Niederlassung

Eine weitere Sofabar am Gärtnerplatz; Sonntag gibt's Tatort

Another Sofa bar at the Gärtnerplatz; You can watch the famous "Tatort" live on Sundays there

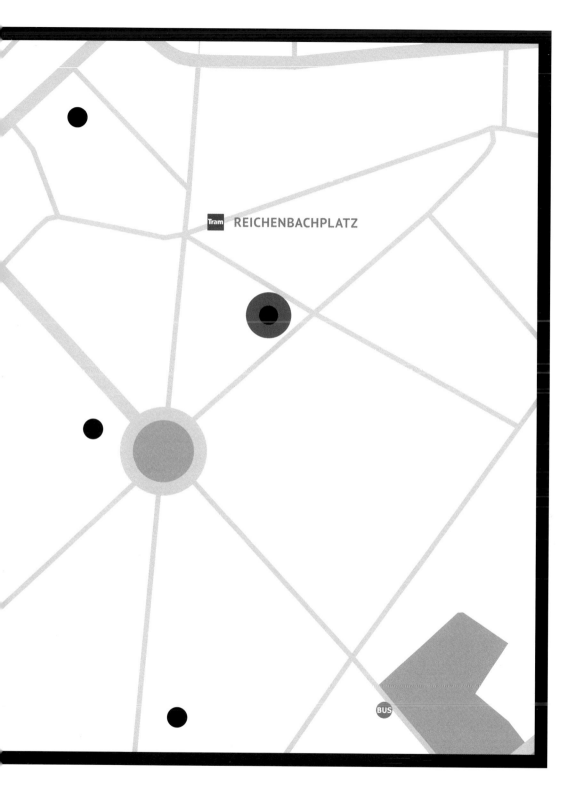

LOCATION Buttermelcherstraße 6, 80469 München • **PHONE** +49 (0)89 32600307
WEB www.niederlassung.org • **MAIL** info@niederlassung.org

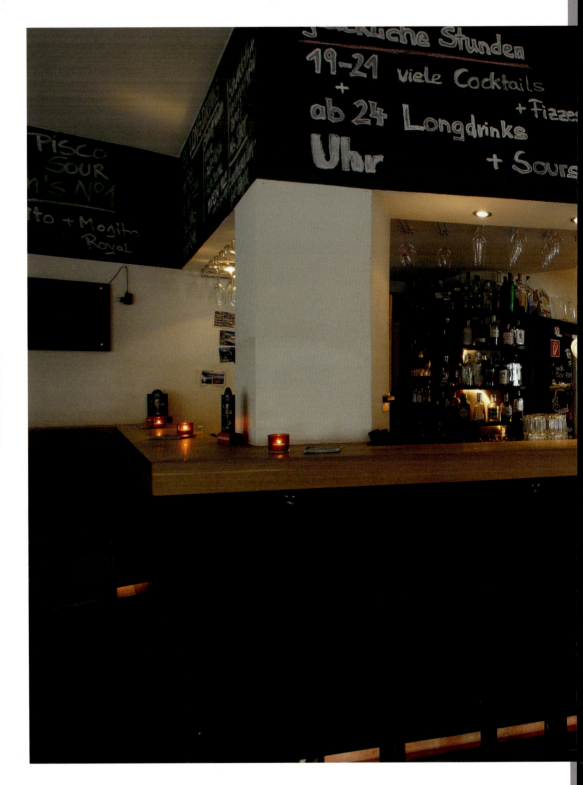

NIEDERLASSUNG

Panther

Internationales Publikum; Bar mit Fisch Fleisch im Angebot; Edles Ambiente und entspannte Stimmung; Hausgemachte Schokoladen-Parfaits probieren
International Bar with fish and meat on offer; Elegant setting and relaxed atmosphere; Try Homemade Chocolate Bars

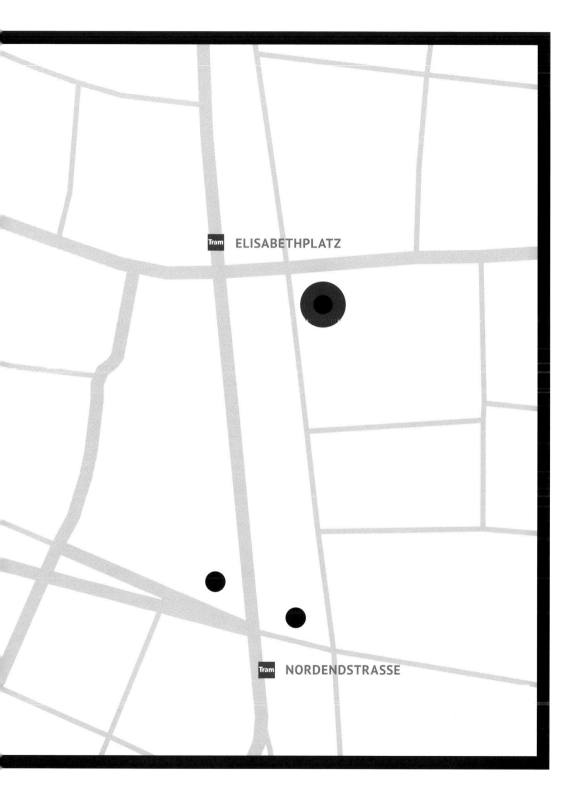

LOCATION Franz-Joseph-Straße 45, 80801 München • PHONE +49 (0)89 273 727 50
WEB panther-grill.de • MAIL info@panther-grill.de

W XYZ Bar

Teure, entspannte Hotelbar direkt am Hauptbahnhof; Gemischtes Publikum; Eher gediegen; Sehr freundliches Personal; Angenehme, ruhige Atmosphäre; Ideal für den Feierabend

Expensive, relaxed hotel bar directly at the main station; Mixed audience; Rather dignified; Very friendly staff; Pleasant, quiet atmosphere; Ideal for after work drinks

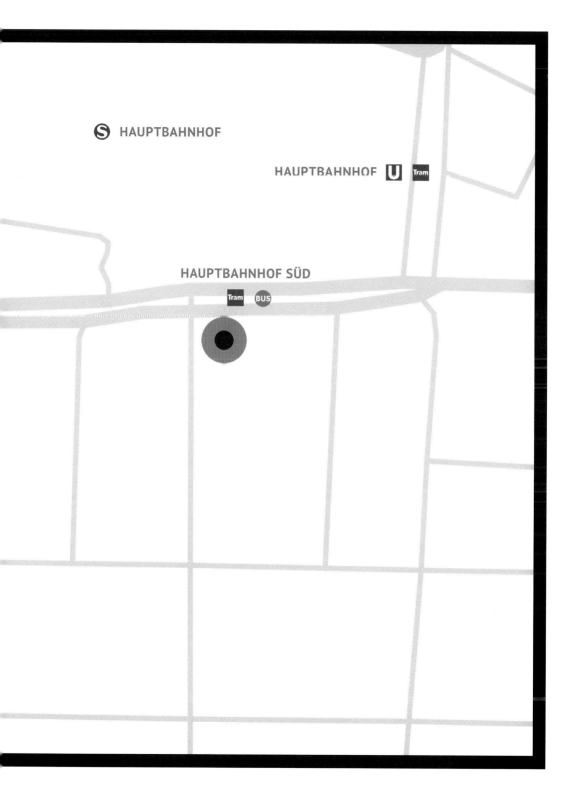

LOCATION Bayerstraße 37, 80335 München • **PHONE** +49 (0)89 540 237 0
WEB www.aloftmunichhotel.com • **MAIL** info.munich@alofthotels.com

W XYZ BAR

Zephyr Bar

Bedürfnis und Kunst sollen zusammenfinden; Flash Dance und ein fliegender Teppich sind immer vor Ort; Genießer sind hier richtig; Sehr professionelle Barkeeper mit viel Liebe zum Detail

Needs and art should come together; Flashdance and a flying carpet are always on the spot; Enjoy!; Very professional bartender with great attention to detail

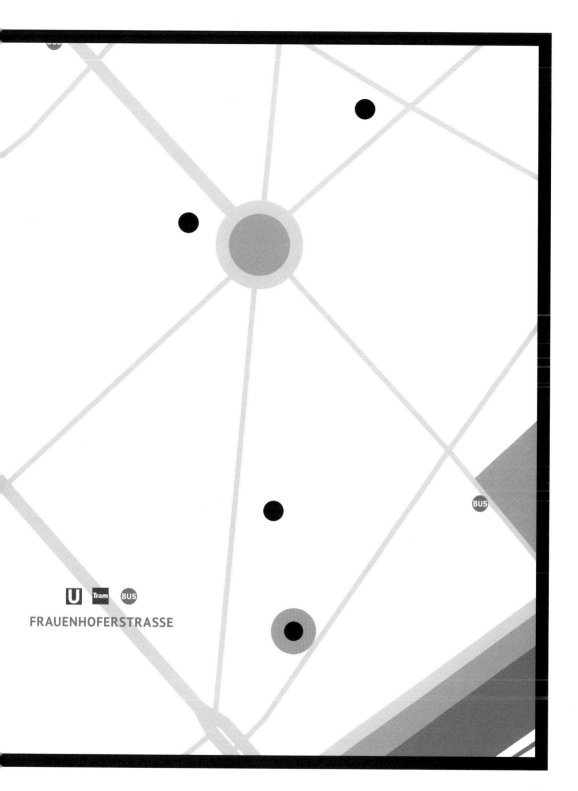

LOCATION Baaderstraße 68, 80469 München • PHONE +49 (0)173 599 53 35
WEB www.zephyr-bar.de • MAIL info@zephyr-bar.de

Das Provi-sorium

Provisorische Bar in einem Laden mit Cafe; Partyvolk; Minimalismus; Kunst
Provisional bar in a shop with cafe; party people; Minimalism; Art

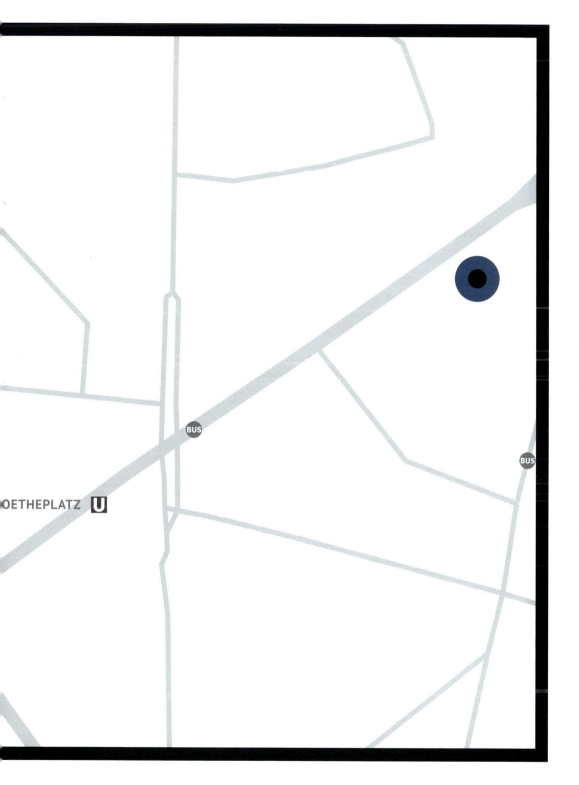

LOCATION Lindwurmstraße 37, 80337 München • PHONE +49 (0)162 749 590 5

DAS PROVISORIUM

Skybar

Coole Flughafenlounge; Internationales Publikum; Dank großen Panoramafenstern kann man das Treiben auf dem Rollfeld beobachten; Erstaunlich große Getränkeauswahl; Sehr modernes Ambiente

Cool airport lounge; International audience; Thanks to large windows you can watch the action on the runway; Amazingly great selection of drinks; Very modern atmosphere

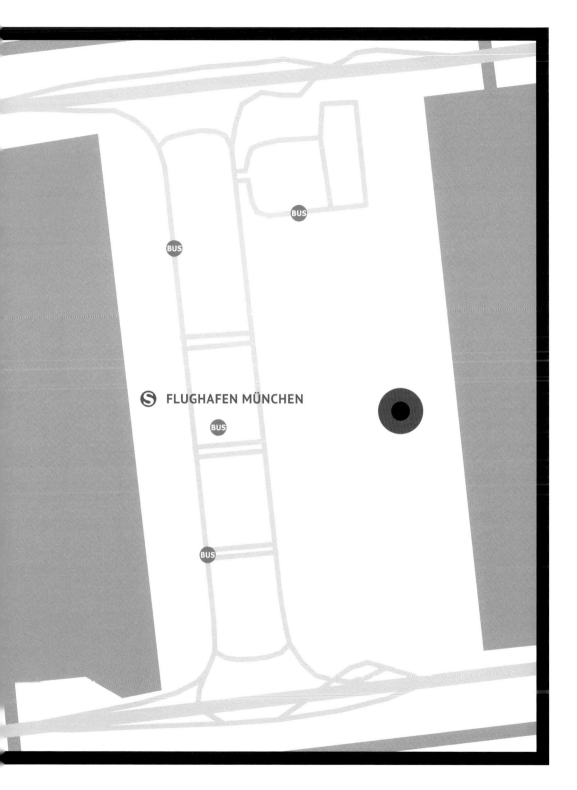

LOCATION Flughafen München (MUC), Oberding • **PHONE** +49 (0)69 86 799 799
WEB www.lufthansa.com

Freebird Bar

Leckere Cocktails in easy going-Atmosphäre; Stylisch; Lynyrd Skynyrd war der Namenspatron

Delicious cocktails in easy going atmosphere; Stylish; Lynyrd Skynyrd was the patron name

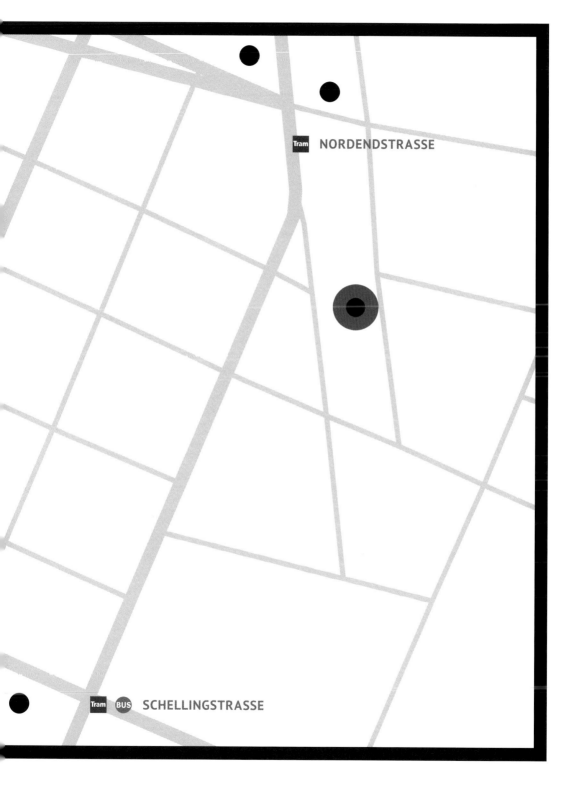

LOCATION Nordendstraße 12, 80799 München • **PHONE** +49 (0)89 273 745 20
WEB www.freebird-munich.com • **MAIL** mail@freebird-munich.com

FREEBIRD BAR

Oskar Maria Brasserie

Untergebracht im Literaturhaus; Internationales Publikum; Auch tagsüber einen Besuch wert; Leckere Speisen in Kaffeehausatmosphäre; Internationales Publikum – Touristen mischen sich mitKulturinteressierten

Accomodated in the Literaturhaus; International audience; Also worth a visit during the day; Delicious food in coffee house atmosphere; International audience – tourists mingle with those interested in culture

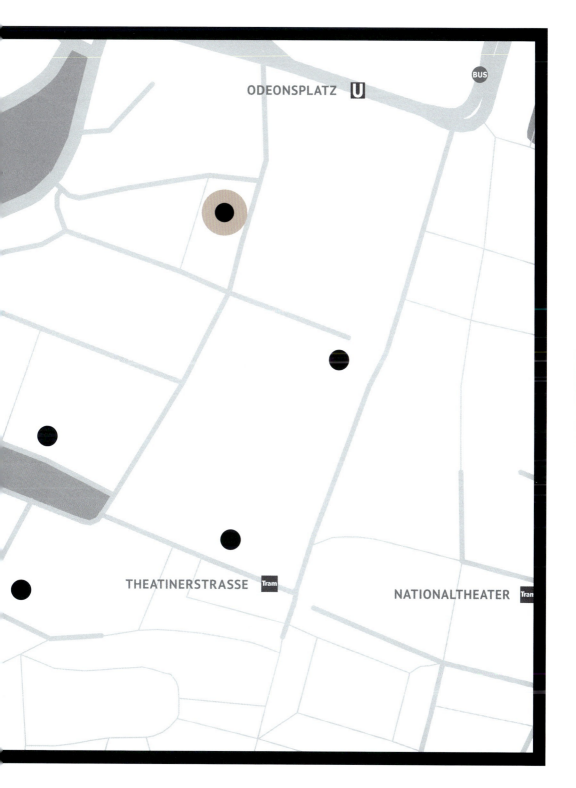

LOCATION Salvatorplatz 1, 80333 München • **PHONE** +49(0)89 291 960 29
WEB www.oskarmaria.com • **MAIL** info@oskar-maria.de

OSKAR MARIA BRASSERIE

Schumann's Tagesbar

Gediegener Tagestreff, um einen Kaffee mit feinem Kuchen zu genießen. Oder schon den ersten Aperitif; Eine Café-Bar, ein Treffpunkt vor der Arbeit, um den Tag anzugehen. Oder zum Lunch oder Aperitif; Die Schumann's Tagesbar ist einfach eine internationale Bar, wie es sie in jeder Großstadt geben muss

Classical bar for the daytime, to enjoy a coffee with fine cakes. Or the first aperitif; A cafe bar, meeting point before work to start the day. Or to take Lunch or appetizer; The Schumann's Tagesbar is an international bar, that fits in any bigger City in the world

LOCATION Maffeistraße 6, 80333 München • PHONE +49(0)89 242 177 00
WEB www.schumanns.de • MAIL info@schumanns.de

Vega Bar

Panoramafenster; Ledercouch; Blumentapeten sind herrlich; Sonntag und Montag geschlossen; Tarantino lässt grüßen; Hipster und Nachbarn feiern hier zusammen

Panoramic window; Leather couch; Flowers are beautiful; Closed on Sundays and Mondays; Greetings from Tarantino; Hipsters and neighbors celebrate together here

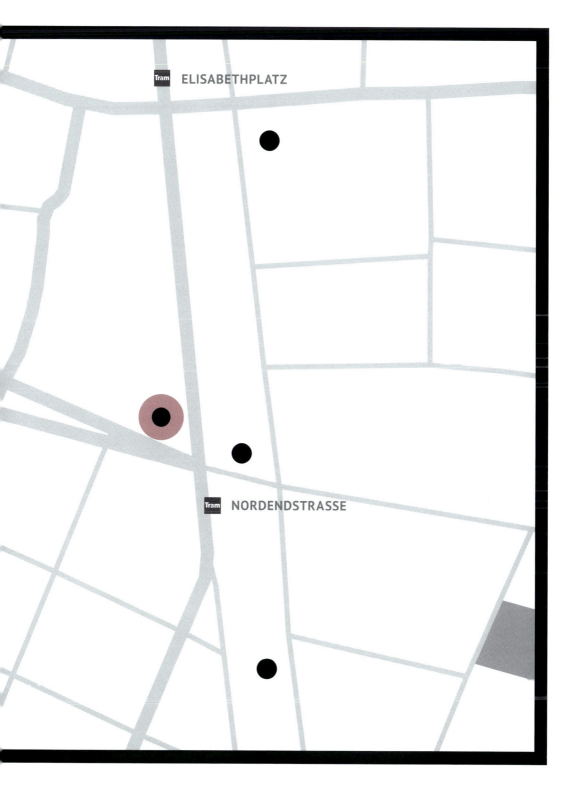

LOCATION Georgenstraße 56, 80799 München • PHONE +49 (0)89 121 388 391
WEB www.vega-bar.de • MAIL info@vega-bar.de

Schu-
mann's

„Kein Kommentar nötig" | *"No comment required"* – Charles Schumann

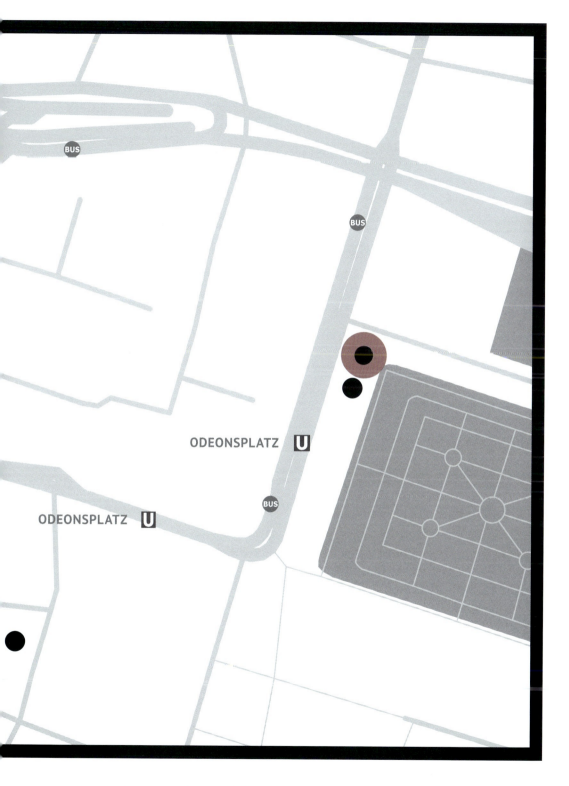

LOCATION Odeonsplatz 6-7, 80539 München • **PHONE** +49(0)89 229060
WEB www.schumanns.de • **MAIL** info@schumanns.de

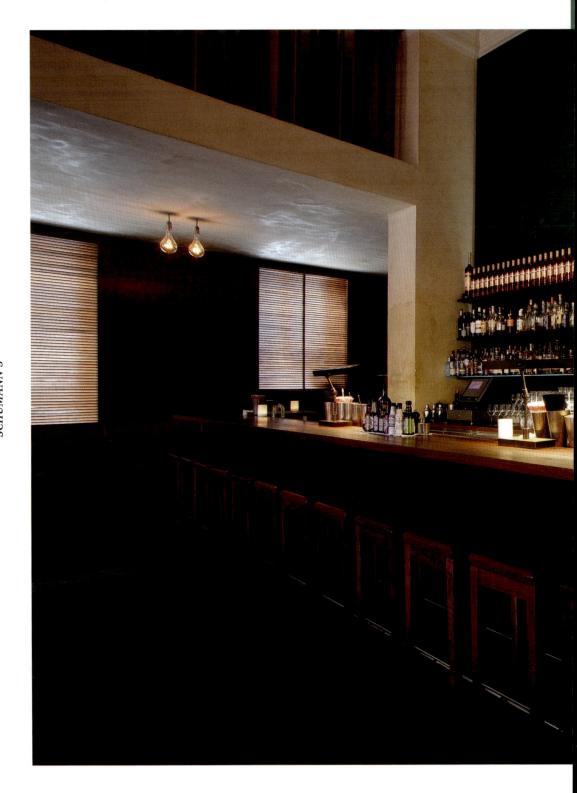

Leonardo Royal Hotel

Hotelbar; Elegant eingerichtet; Sehr leckeres Clubsandwich; Direkt am Olympiapark

Hotel bar; Elegantly furnished; Very delicious club sandwich; Directly at the Olympia park

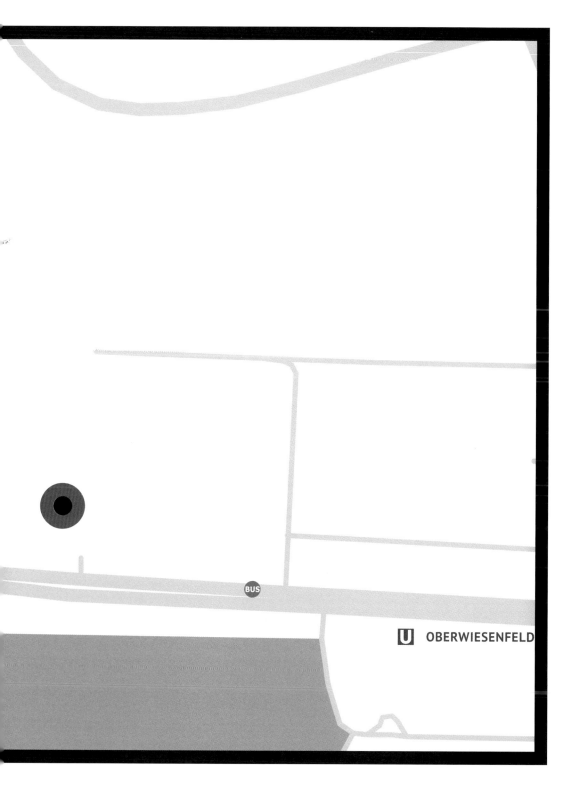

LOCATION Moosacher Straße 90, 80809 München • **PHONE** +49 (0)89 288 538 0
WEB www.leonardo-hotels.com • **MAIL** info.royalmunich@leonardo-hotels.com

Le Florida

Food & Drinks mit bisschen Tam-Tam; Leckere Burger; Kleine Cocktailkarte; Ein schöner Start in den Abend in Schwabing
Food & Drinks with Chi Chi; Delicious burgers; Small cocktail card; One fine start to the evening in Schwabing

LOCATION Georgenstraße 48, 80799 München • **PHONE** +49 (0)89 444 29 555
WEB www.leflorida.de • **MAIL** info@leflorida.de

LE FLORIDA

Helene

Mischung zwischen Bar, Disco und Loungerestaurant; Oben essen unten tanzen; Direkt gegenüber vom Vereinsheim in der Occamstraße; Riesen Fenster mit schönem Blick auf die Schwabinger Flaneure; Sehr motiviertes Team; Leckeres Essen aus dem Nahen Osten; Helene ist eben halt doch auch die kleine Schwester vom Schmock in der Augustenstraße

Mix between a bar, disco and Lounge Restaurant; Eat upstairs, dance down stairs; Opposite the Vereinsheim in Occam street; Giant windows with beautiful views of the Schwabing strollers; Very motivated team; Delicious food from the Middle East; Helene is just the little sister of the Schmock in Augustenstraße

LOCATION Occamstraße 5, 80802 München • **PHONE** +49 (0)89 740 352 09
WEB www.helene-muenchen.de • **MAIL** hello@helene-muenchen.de

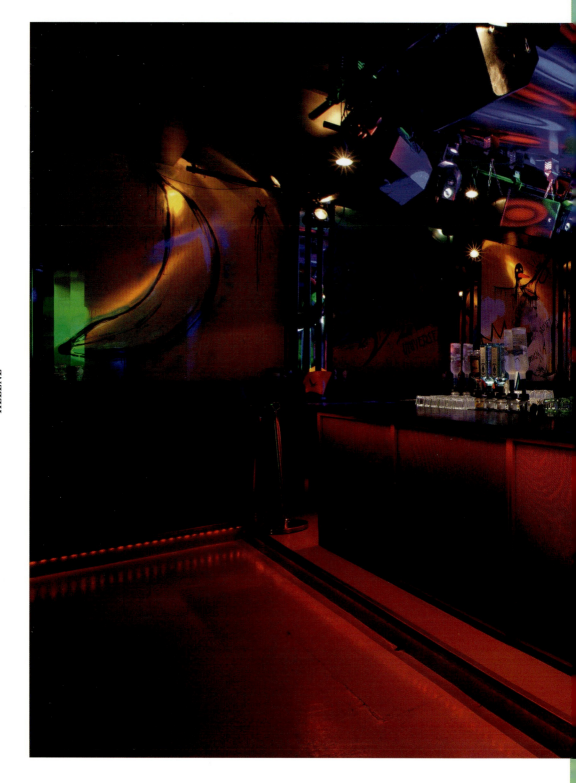

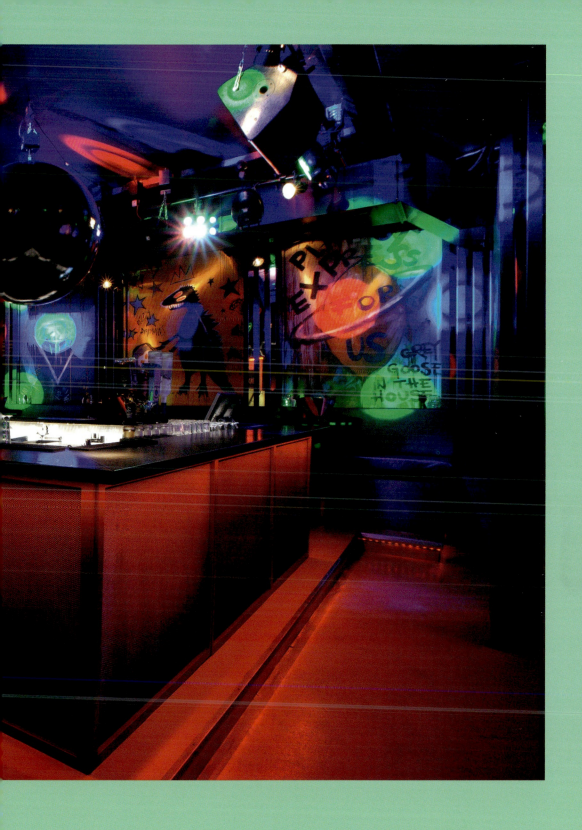

Munich Palace Hotel

5 Sterne Boutique Hotel mit Bar; Wunderschöne, klassische Hotelbar mit internationalem Publikum; Familienbetrieb der Gastrofamily Kufler; Direkt am Friedensengel; Ein guter Start in die Nacht

5 star Boutique hotel with bar; Beautiful, classic hotel bar with an international audience; Family business of the Kuflers; Located at Friedensengel; A good start into the night

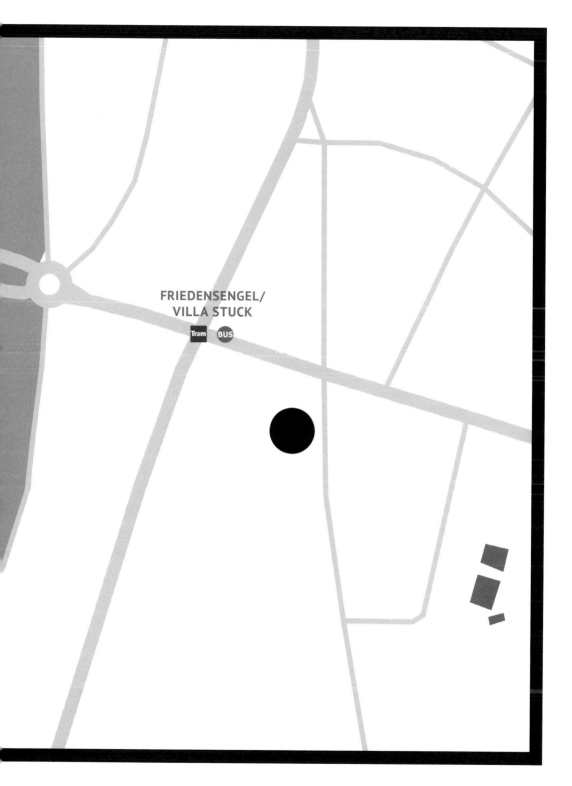

LOCATION Trogerstraße 21, 81675 München • PHONE +49 (0)89 418 710
WEB hotel-muenchen-palace.de • MAIL info@hotel-muenchen-palace.de

MUNICH PALACE HOTEL

Kiste

Alkohol; Kunst und Musik; Welch schönes Konzept!; Keine Karten; Keine Reservierung; Einfach vorbei schauen; Leider nur noch zwei Jahre

Alcohol; Art and music; What a beautiful concept!; No menu; No reservation; Just take a look; Unfortunately just two years of existence

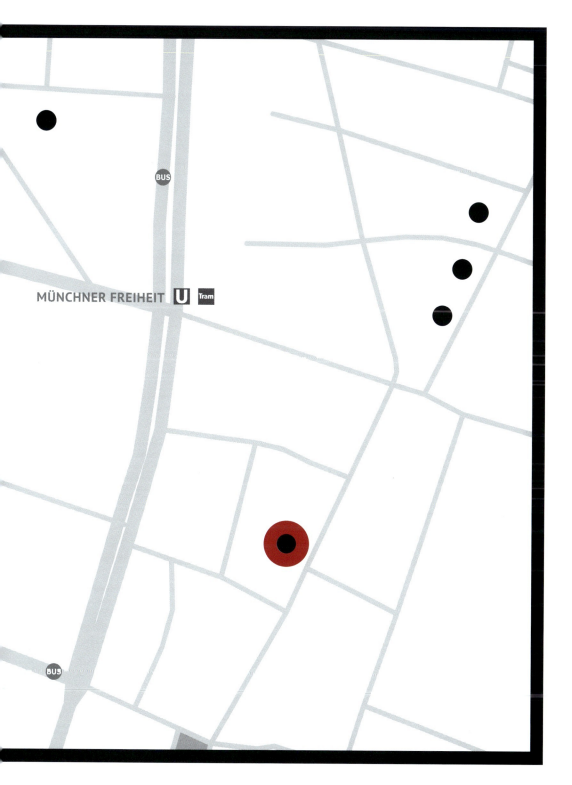

LOCATION Siegesstraße 17, 80802 München • **PHONE** +49 (0)89 740 317 54
WEB www.indiekiste.de • **MAIL** kontakt@indiekiste.de

KISTE

Wedding Chapel

Schummrig, happy tropical; Aus dem ehemaligen Pop-As entwickelt sich ein neuer Pilspub-Szenetreff für Hipster; Münchner Biere gibt es hier nicht; Eigentlich wollen die Besitzer nicht, dass jeder ihre Bar kennt. Zum Glück für uns gibt es das Wort „eigentlich"

Cheerful, happy tropical; A new Pitspub hot spot developed from the former pop-As for Hipsters; There are no Munich beers here; Actually the owners don't want everyone to know their bar. Fortunately for us there is the word "actually"

LOCATION Thalkirchner Straße 12, 80337 München

WEDDING CHAPEL

Ben's Bar

Karibik Style; Cocktails aus Kuba; Sehr viel Lebensfreude; Direkt in Schwabing bei der U-Bahn Station Münchner Freiheit; Gewinner des Gastro-Awards in der Kategorie Cocktails, auch wenn das schon ein paar Jahre her ist; Dienstags und Freitags den ganzen Abend Happy hour; Burger gibt's auch

Caribbean Style; Cocktails from Cuba; A lot of joy; Located at the subway station Münchner Freiheit; Winner of the Gastro-Award in the Cocktails category, even if it has already made a few years here; The whole evenings of Tuesdays and Fridays, Happy hour; There are burgers too

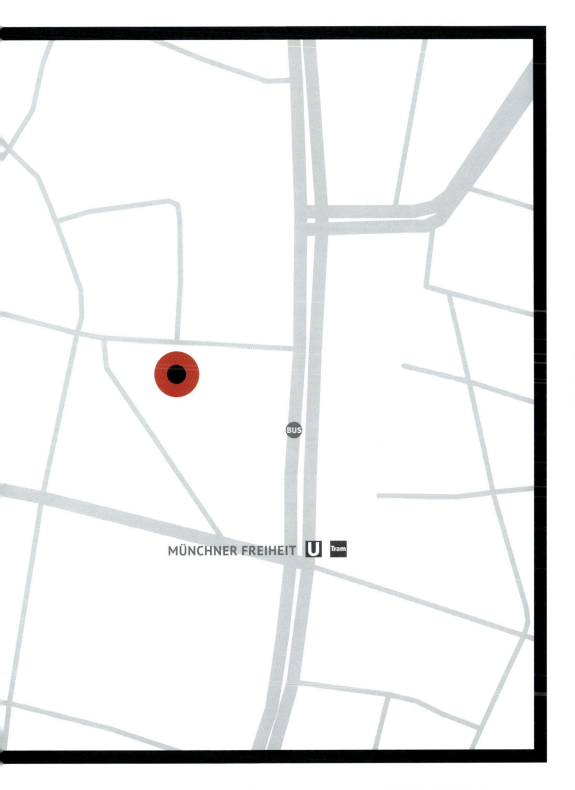

LOCATION Clemensstraße 7, 80803 München • **PHONE** +49 (0)89 289 709 19
WEB www.bens-bar.de • **MAIL** info@bens-bar.de

BEN'S BAR

Salon Irkutsk

Bar, Konzerte, Kunst und natürlich auch was zum Trinken; Das Abendbistro für den geselligen Trinksport; Das Wirteteam stammt aus Russland und Frankreich: Schöner kann man Völkerverständigung kaum feiern; Freitags Kunstsalon, montags Pianostage; Gut so

Bar, Concerts, Art and of course also for drinking; The evening bar for the sociable drinking sport; The hosts team comes from Russia and France: More beautifully, one can hardly celebrate international understanding; Fridays Art Salon, mondays Piano days; OK then

LOCATION Isabellastraße 4, 80798 München • PHONE +49(0)179 217 575 30
WEB www.salonirkutsk.de

SALON IRKUTSK

Schwarzer Engel

Endlich eine Bar mit E-Guitarren an der Wand; Hart, aber herrlich; Ausprobieren!

Finally a bar with electric guitars on the wall; Hard, but gorgeous; Try it out!

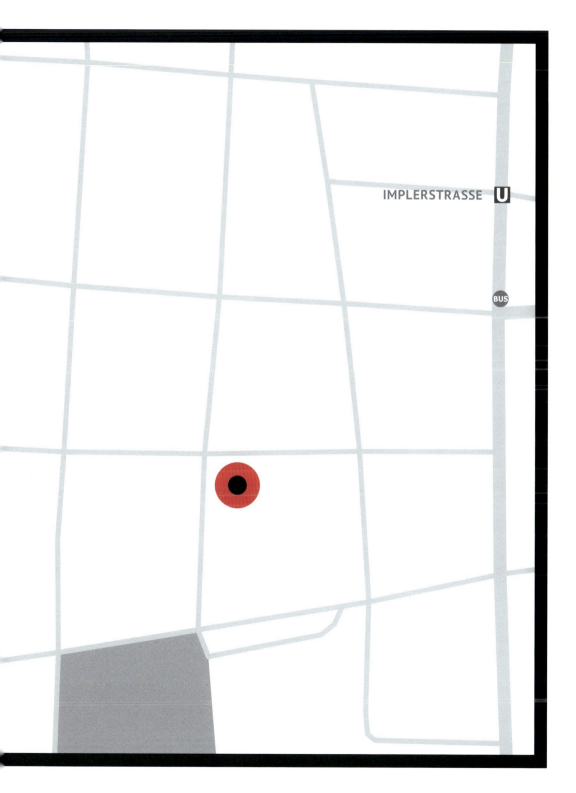

LOCATION Lindenschmitstraße 9, 81371 München • **PHONE** +49 (0)89 590 687 55

SCHWARZER ENGEL

Cabaret Pigalle

Ehemalige Table Dance-Bar; Viel Charme, dank der alten Einrichtung; Direkt im Schlachthofviertel; Auch ältere Semester feiern hier noch gerne bis in die Morgenstunden; Die Stangen dürfen bespielt werden

Former table dance bar; Lots of charm. Thanks to the old Setup; Located in the Meatpacking District; Older generations still like to party until the morning hours here; Try the Pole Dance

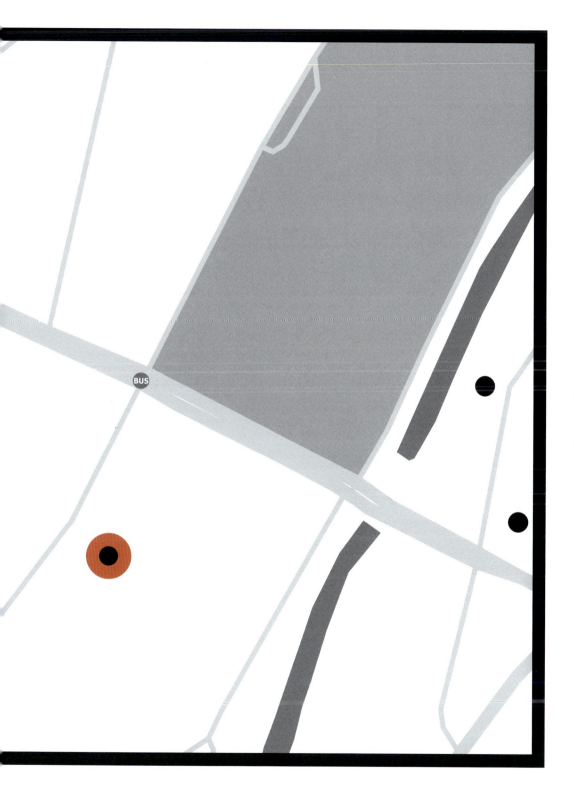

LOCATION Thalkirchner Straße 23, 80337 München • **PHONE** +49 (0)172 793 068 2
WEB www.pigalle-muenchen.de • **MAIL** info@pigalle-muenchen.de

CABARET PIGALLE

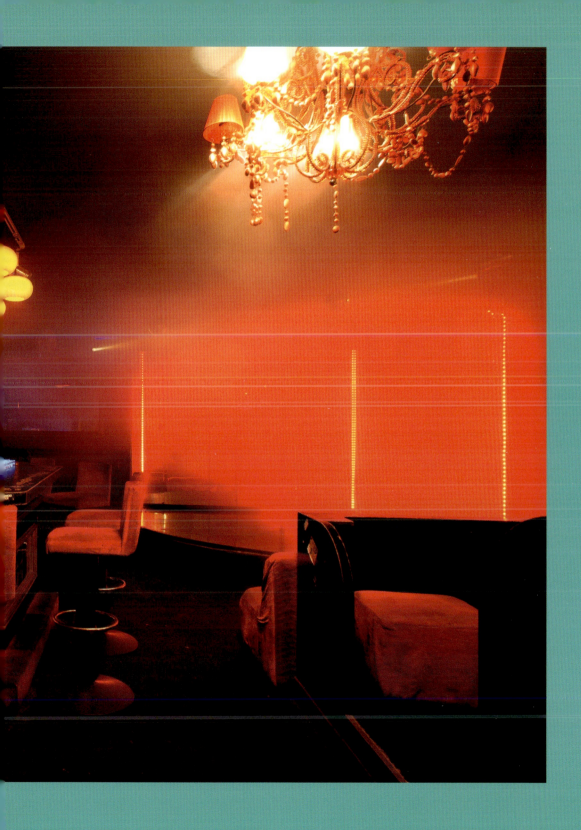

Robinson's Bar

Discokugel mit an Board!; Kreide und schwarze Wände; Hier wird gefeiert, getrunken und geschwitzt; Meist recht voll; Sehr beliebt; Ehemalige Kölschkneipe nun Münchner Szenetreff; Bis 5 Uhr morgens für Party bereit

Disco ball with you on board!; Chalk and black walls; Here we celebrate, drink and sweat; Usually quite full; Very popular; Former Kölsch pub, now Munich's hot spot; Ready for party till 5am

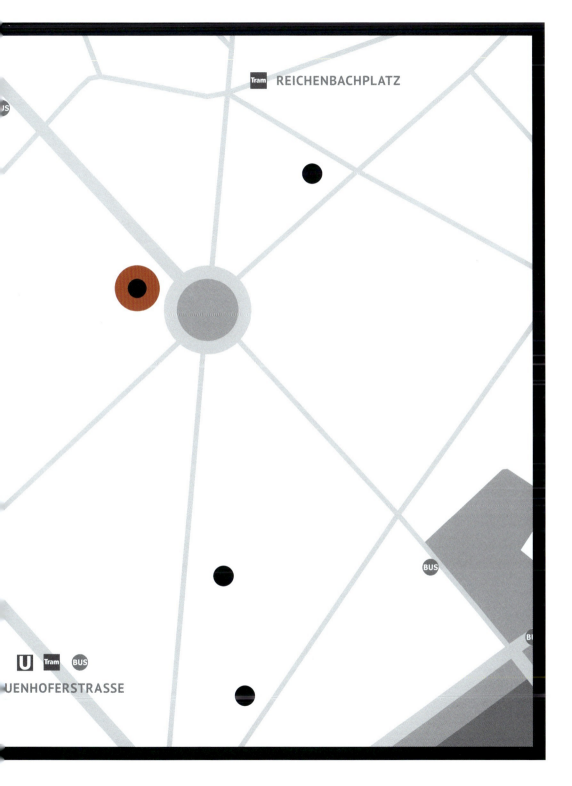

LOCATION Corneliusstraße 14, 80469 München • PHONE +49 (0)172 86 61 6 86
WEB www.robinsonkuhlmann.com • MAIL robinson@robinsonkuhlmann.com

Kammer-spiele Bar

Eröffnete am 16.9.2016. Ein voller Erfolg. Es gab kaum ein Durchkommen Publikum: Künstler, Schauspieler der Kammerspiele und freaky People, die in der Nähe ihres Luxushotels in der Maximilianstrasse zum ehrlichen Feiern suchen; Alter von 25 bis 45; Hier gibt es zur Förderung der Völkerverständigung sogar gemischte Toiletten; Und wer wenig Geld hat, kann sich auf der Toilette für 2,00 € ein Überraschungsbier aus einem Automaten rauslassen

Opened on 16.9.2016. A complete success. It was hard to get through Audience: artist, actors of the intimate theatre and freaky people, who are looking for celebrations near their luxury hotel in Maximilian street; Age from 25 to 45 years; There are even mixed toilets for promoting international understanding; And someone with little money can get a surprise beer for 2.00 € at the beermachine in the washing room

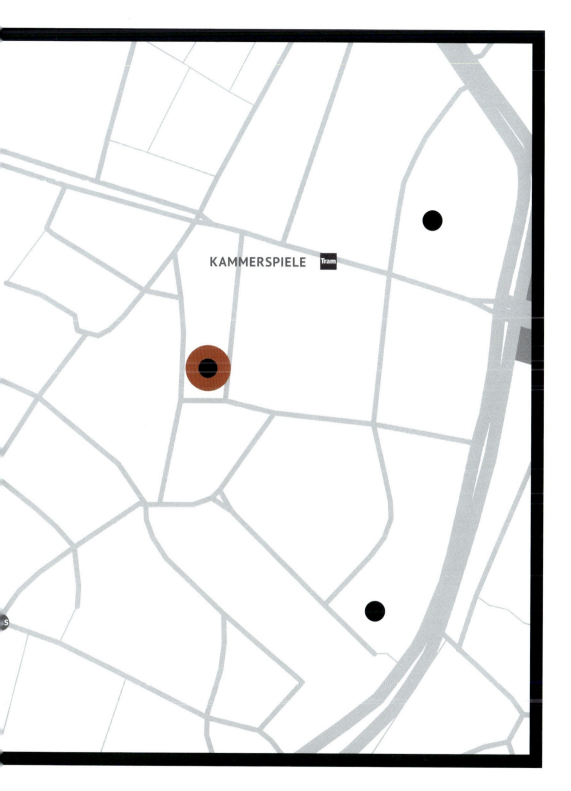

LOCATION Falckenbergstraße 1, 80539 München • **PHONE** +49 (0)89 233 368 20
WEB www.muenchner-kammerspiele.de • **MAIL** bar@kammerspiele.de

KAMMERSPIELE BAR

Cohibar City

Älteste Lateinamerikanische Bar in München; DJs bringen die Gäste in Stimmung; Mehrfach ausgezeichnete Cocktails; Gemischtes, in der Regel sehr lebens- und tanzfreudiges Publikum; Manchmal gibt's sogar spontane Tanzeinlagen, die einen an From Dusk Till Dawn erinnern; Am Wochenende bieten die Barkeeper die fast schon legendäre Live-Bartender Show

The oldest Latin American bar in Munich; DJs put the guests in the mood; Multiple cocktails; Mixed, generally very lively and dance-loving audience; Sometimes there are even spontaneous dance routines which brings memories; From Dusk Till Dawn; On weekends, the bartenders offer the almost legendary live bartender show

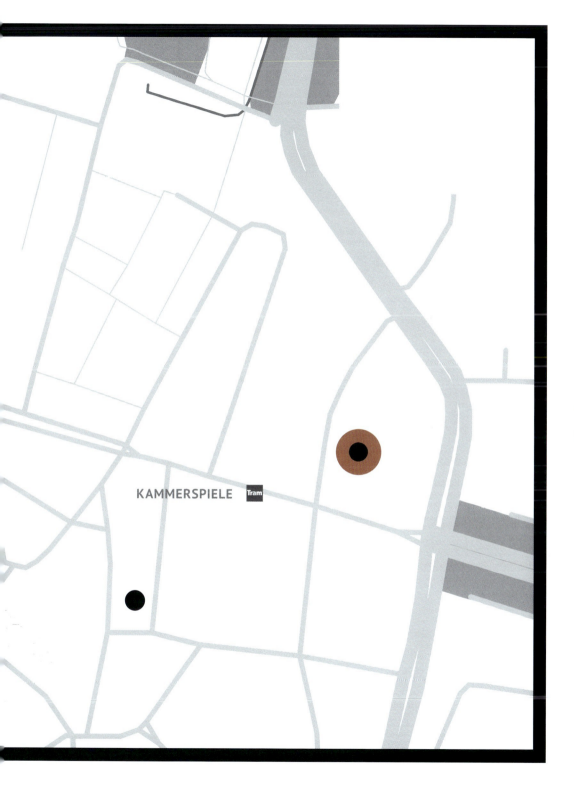

LOCATION Herzog-Rudolf-Straße 2, 80539 München • **PHONE** +49 (0)89 22 880 289
WEB www.cohibar-city.com • **MAIL** info@cohibar-city.com

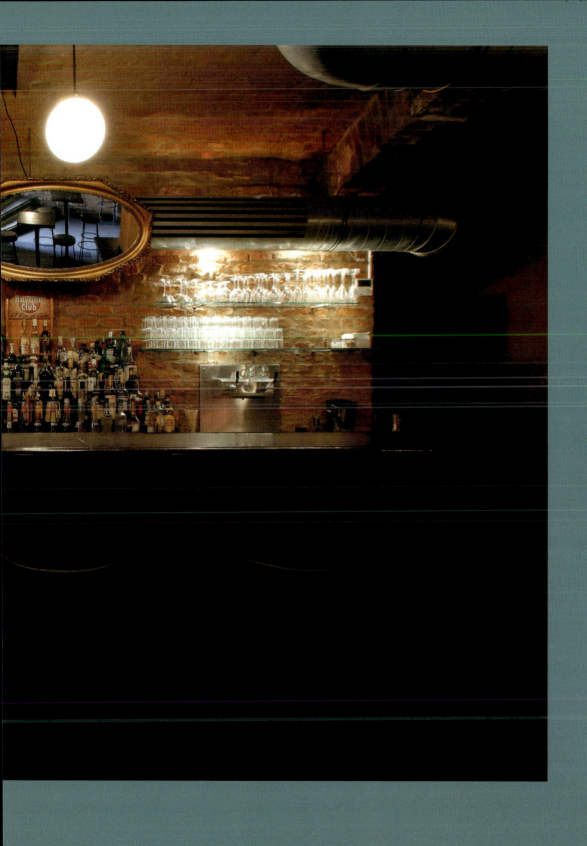

Champagne Characters

Der Name ist Programm; Hier gibt es eine Riesenauswahl für Freunde des alkoholischen Blubbergetränks: Champagner in Hülle und Fülle; Auch ausgefallene und seltene Marken; Dazu ein paar gemütliche Sofas und gut ist

The name says it all; There is a huge selection for fans of alcoholic bubbling drinks: Champagne in abundance; Also unusual and rare brands; A couple of cozy sofas make the perfect place

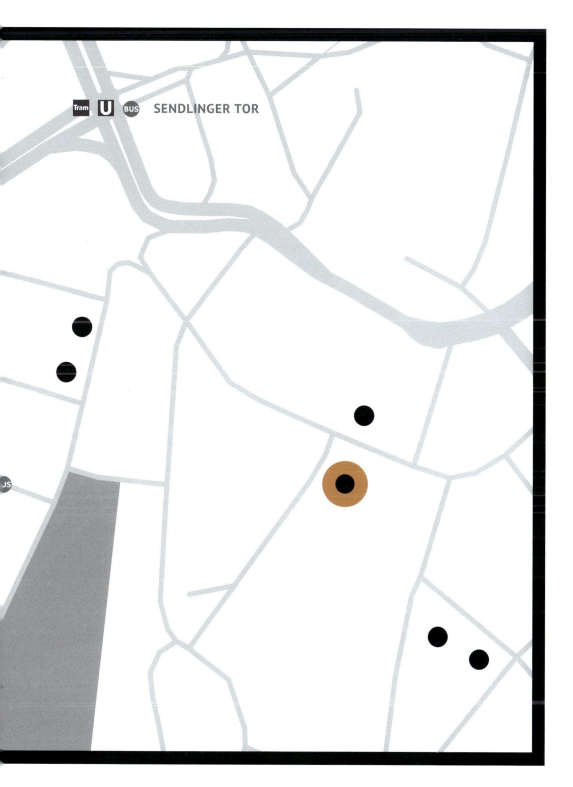

LOCATION Holzstraße 1, 80469 München • **PHONE** +49 (0)89 287 481 17
WEB www.champagne-characters.com • **MAIL** nicola@champagne-characters.com

CHAMPAGNE CHARACTERS

L'Aperitivo

Italien erleben; Spritz als Bestseller; Es wird auch nach den Öffnungszeiten weiter gefeiert – Einfach klopfen

Experience Italy; Spritz at its best; It remains lively after the opening hours – Just knock

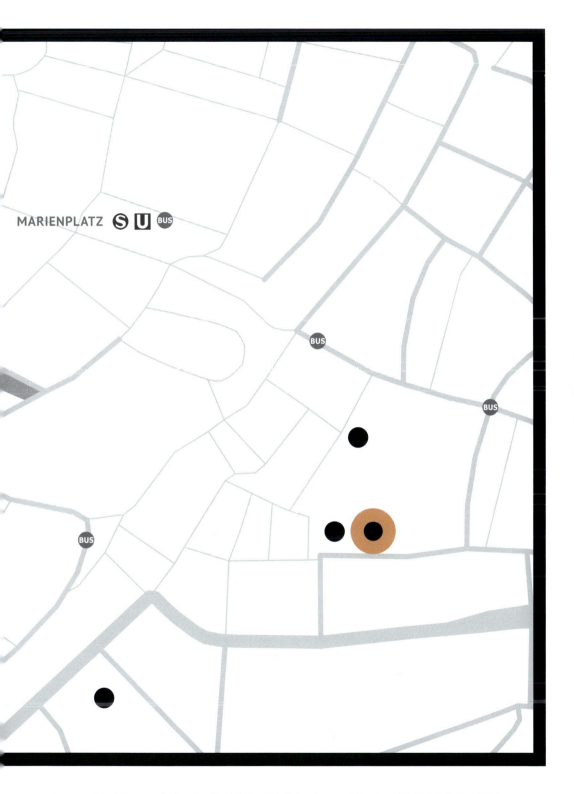

LOCATION Westenriederstraße 13, 80331 München • **PHONE** +49 (0)89 123 06 580
WEB www.laperitivo.de • **MAIL** info@laperitivo.de

MUC-Bar

Bar mit Metallscherensschnitt der Münchner Skyline; Tolle Aussicht; Das ehemalige Marktstadl; Direkt am Viktualienmarkt; Ist nicht vergessen aber nun doch mit dem Einzug der MUC Bar sehr viel freundlicher gestaltet; Viele Drinks und verschiedene Biere in wunderschönem Holzambiente

Bar with a shear cut of the Munich skyline; Great view; The former Marktstadl; Located in the Viktualienmarkt; Is not forgotten however with the more friendly structures, the MUC bar is gaining popularity; Lots of drinks and various beers in a beautiful wooden setting

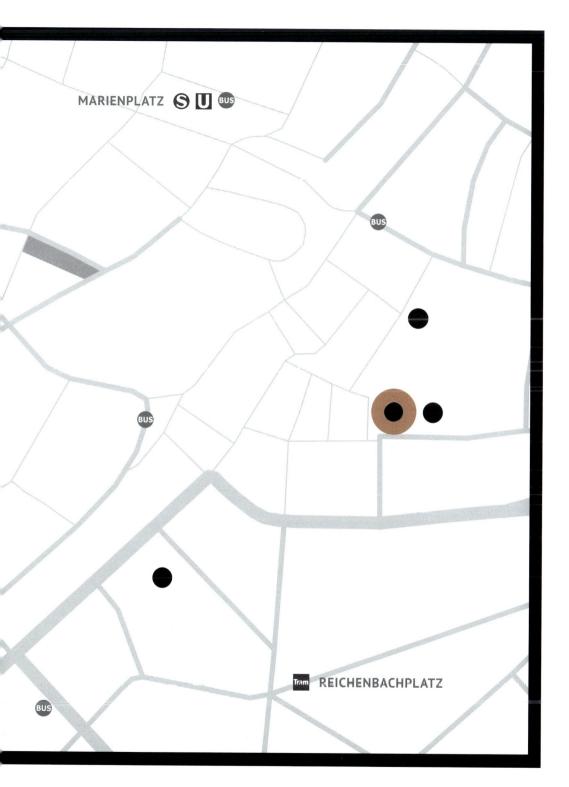

LOCATION Westenriederstraße 13, 80331 München • PHONE +49 (0)89 294 010
WEB www.muc-bar.de • MAIL info@muc-bar.de

Benko Bar

Wein, Cocktails und Gemütlichkeit; Backsteinambiente mit Industriecharme; Sofas und Barhocker; Hier findet sich meistens noch ein Platz
Wine, cocktails and coziness; Brick setting with industrial charm; Sofas and bar stools; Many still find room here

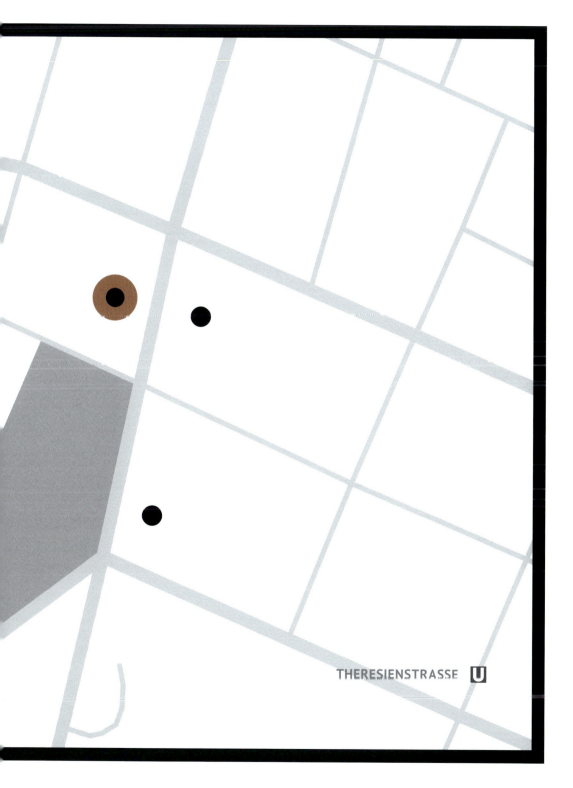

LOCATION Schleißheimer Str. 43, 80797 München • **PHONE** +49(0)89 95 443 618
WEB www.benko-bar.de • **MAIL** hello@benko-bar.de

BENKO BAR

Home

Selbst designte Einrichtung; Tische aus Stahl; Sofas inclusive; Sehr stylisch; Gute Drinks; Faire Preise; Werkstatt-Stil; Gut gemischtes Publikum; Bärte und Tattoos gerne gesehen

Self-designed equipment tables made of steel; Sofas inclusive; Very stylish; Good drinks; Fair prices; Workshop style; Greatly mixed audience; Beards and Tattoos well seen

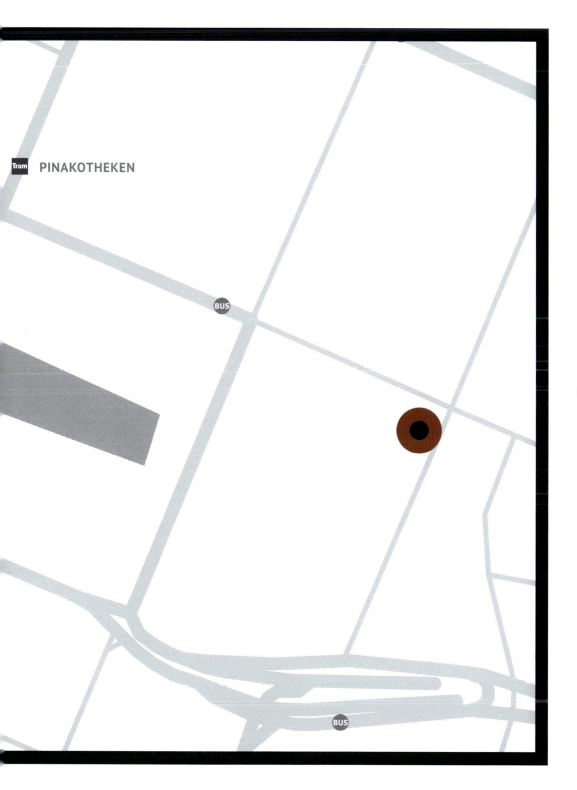

LOCATION Amalienstraße 23, 80333 München

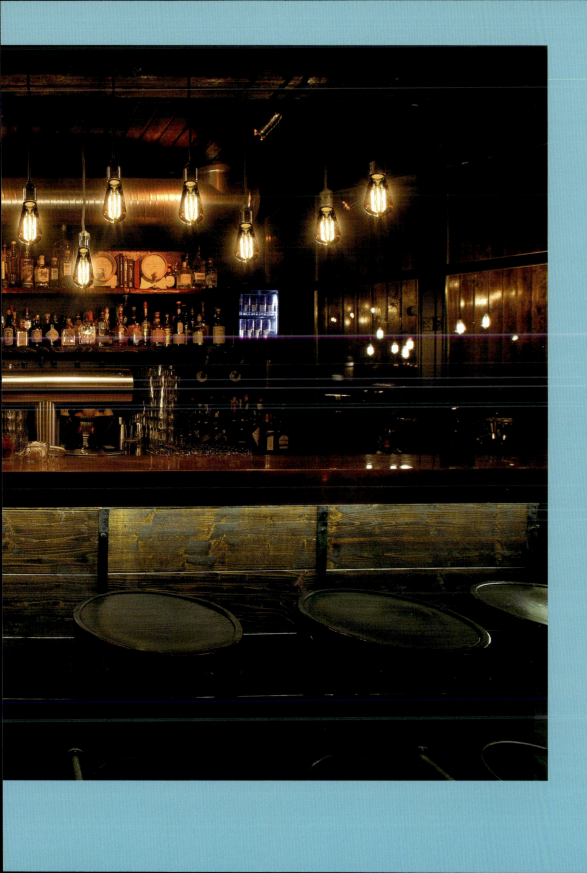

Heilig- geist 1 Bar

Viele Business Leute; Gerne Mittags schon ein Drink; Spezial ist, dass es alle Drinks auch to go gibt

Many business people; A drink in the afternoon with pleasure; Special thing is that you can take all drinks even to go

LOCATION Heiliggeiststraße 1, 80331 München • **PHONE** +49 (0)89 46 229 521
WEB www.heiliggeist1.de • **MAIL** info@heiliggeist1.de

Bucci Bar

Deutsch Italienische Freundschaft; Bunte Mischung an Publikum; Leckeres Essen; Bucci Brüder machen den Abend gelungen; Es wird viel diskutiert, gelacht, geratscht; Einfache, aber funktionale Einrichtung; Das Publikum und das Leben sind hier entscheidend

German Italian hospitality; Colorful mix of audience; Bucci brothers make the evening successful; There is much to debate, laugh, and discuss; Simple but functional facility; The audience and the life are crucial here

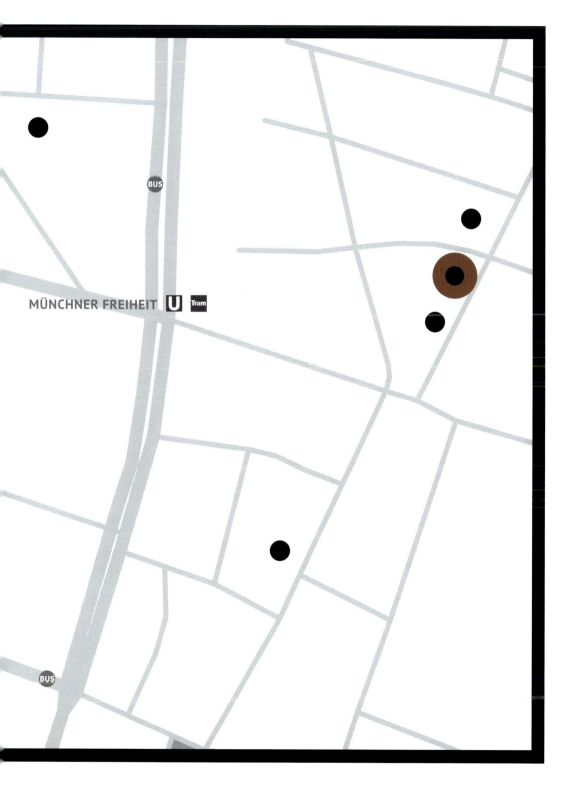

LOCATION Occamstraße 9, 80802 München • PHONE +49(0)89 92 772 603

Les Fleurs du Mal

Und wieder eine Bar von Schumann; Ein über acht Meter langer Tisch verbindet die Gäste; Echter Nussbaum, von Barlegende Charles Schumann selbst erlegt; Tolle Bar; Edle Drinks; Klassisches Publikum: Man nimmt Platz und bespricht die Drinks persönlich mit dem Barmann – wie bei einem Schneider den Anzug

And again a bar from Schumann; An over eight meter long table connects the guests; Real walnut, slayed by the bar legend Charles Schumann himself; Great bar; Fine drinks; Classic audience; One takes a seat and discusses the drinks personally with the bartender – just like at the suit tailor

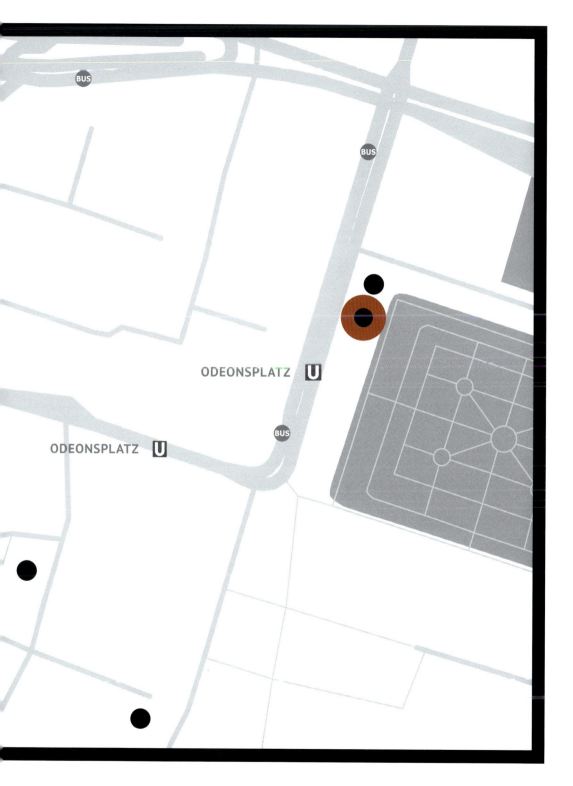

LOCATION Odeonsplatz 6-7, 80539 München • PHONE +49 (0)89 229 060
WEB www.schumanns.de • MAIL info@schumanns.de

LES FLEURS DU MAL

Kooks

Betreutes Trinken… ; Kook bedeutet „der Verrückte"; Matt, der Besitzer ist Kanadier und bietet internationale Biere, wie Kraft-Bier, an; Auch sehr große Wiskey-Auswahl

Supervised drinking… ; Kook means "the crazy"; Matt, the owner is Canadian and offers international beers, such as energy Beer; Also very large wiskey collection

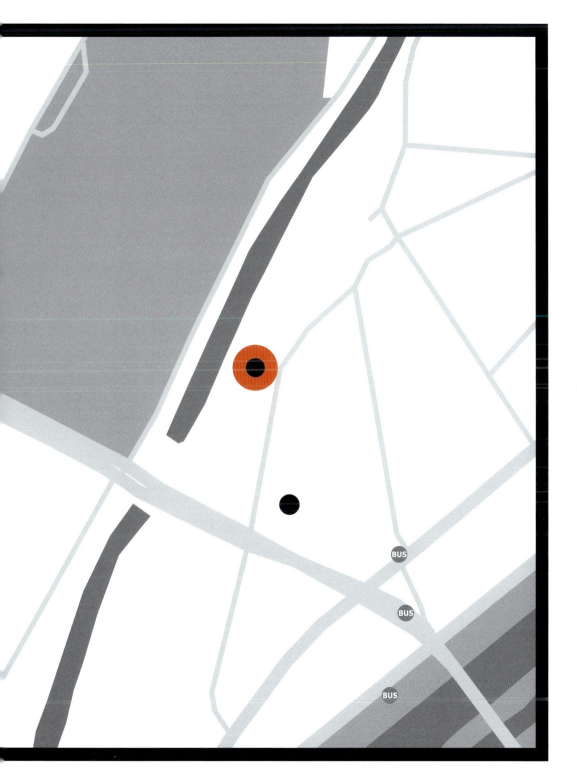

LOCATION Geyerstraße 18, 80469 München • **PHONE** +49 (0)176 98 441 816
WEB www.kooksbar.com

KOOKS

Rattle-snake Saloon

Ein herrliches Münchner Original in Feldmoching; Hier wird Saloon, Country, Rock und Bühnenpower groß gefeiert; Mit der „Rattlesnake" sicher die einzige Bar in München, die ein eigenes Flugzeug besitzt (und eine Eisenbahn über dem Bartresen); Mit kleinem Gastgarten

Delightfully Munich-based, original in Feldmoching; Here Saloon, country, rock and stage Power is a big celebration; With the „Rattlesnake" surely being the only bar in Munich, which has its own aircraft (And a railway over the bar counter); With small garden

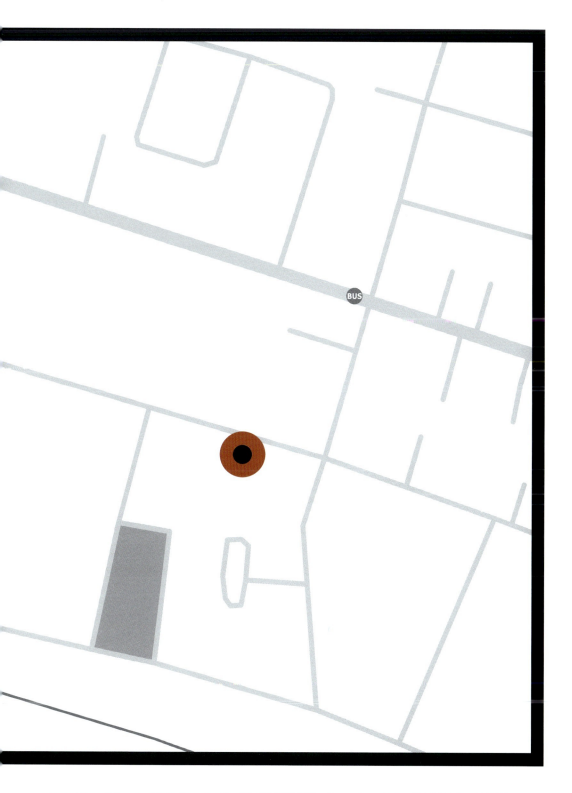

LOCATION Schneeglöckchenstraße 91, 80995 München • **PHONE** +49(0)89 15 04 03 5
WEB www.rattlesnake-saloon.com • **MAIL** bruno@rattlesnake-saloon.com

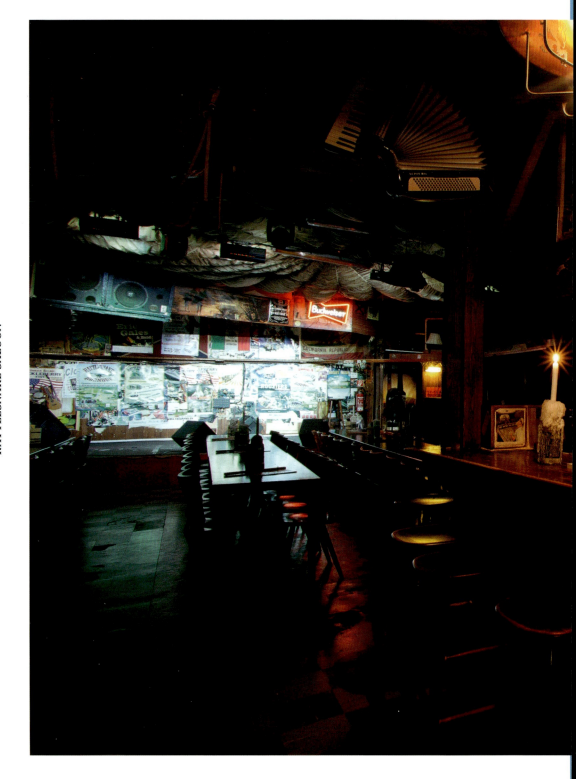

RATTLESNAKE SALOON

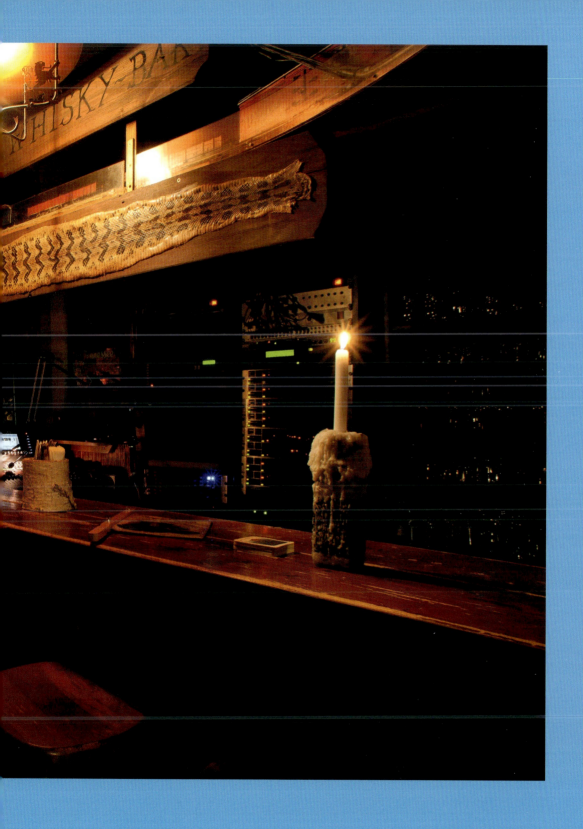

Bruckmann's Bar

Mitten in der Maxvorstadt; Hip, stylisch und dennoch gemütlich; Gold, Holz und leckeres Essen; DJ Tomcraft als Betreiber vor Ort; Summer of Love lässt grüssen

Located in the Maxvorstadt; Hip, stylish and yet comfortable Gold, Wood and delicious food; Has DJ Tomeraft as an operator on the ground; Greetings from summer of love

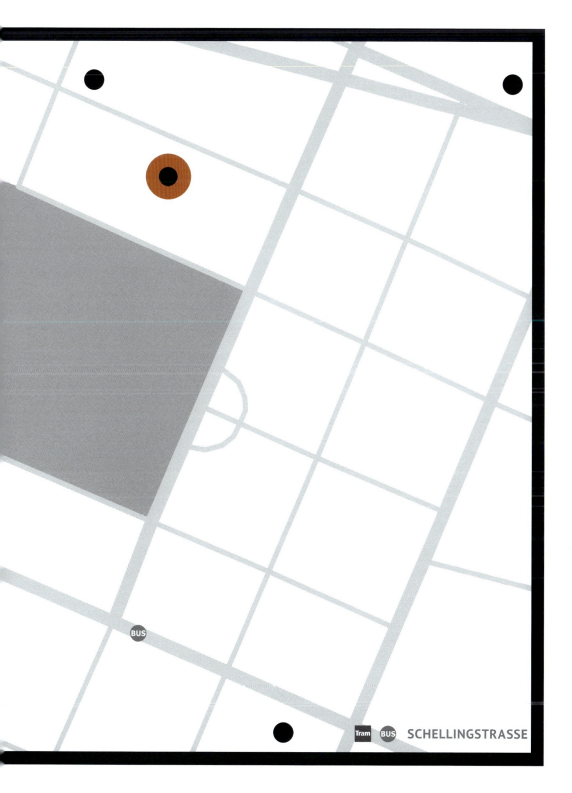

LOCATION Neureutherstraße 21, 80799 München • PHONE +49 (0)89 22 842 895

Heart

Private- und Businessclub im edlen Chic; Szenetreff München; Viele Veranstaltungen; Exzellente Cocktails, viele Parties; Not Members only

Private and business club in elegant chic; Trending meeting place in Munich; Many events; Excellent cocktails, lots of parties; Not a Members only

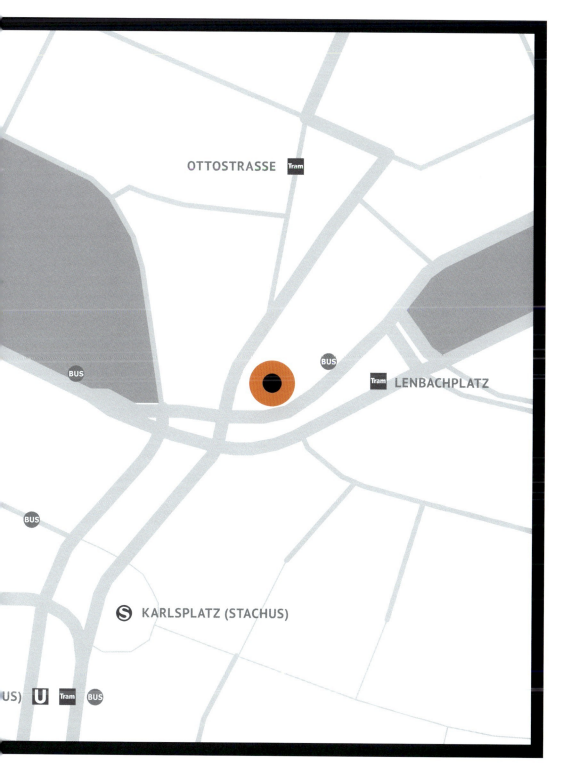

LOCATION Lenbachplatz 2, 80333 München • **PHONE** +49 (0)160 90 900 224
WEB www.h-e-a-r-t.me • **MAIL** hello@h-e-a-r-t.me

HEART

Couch Club

140 Sorten Gin; Gemütliche Sofas in entspannter Atmosphäre; Regelmäßiges Gintasting bis zum Abwinken; Meist gut besucht; Ideal zum Vorglühen

140 types of gin; Cozy couches in a relaxed atmosphere; Regular Gin tasting till you drop; Usually well visited; Ideal for preheating

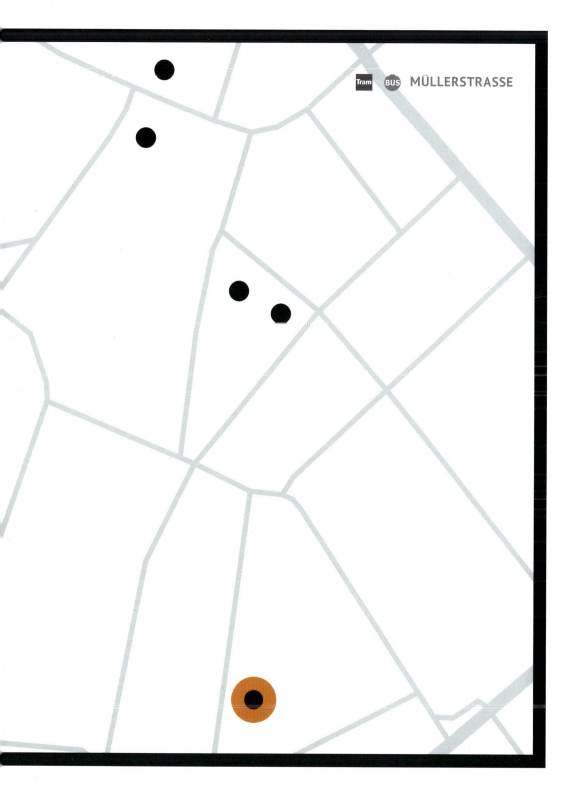

LOCATION Klenzestraße 89, 80469 München • **PHONE** +49 (0)89 12 555 778
WEB www.couch-club.org • **MAIL** info@couch-club.org

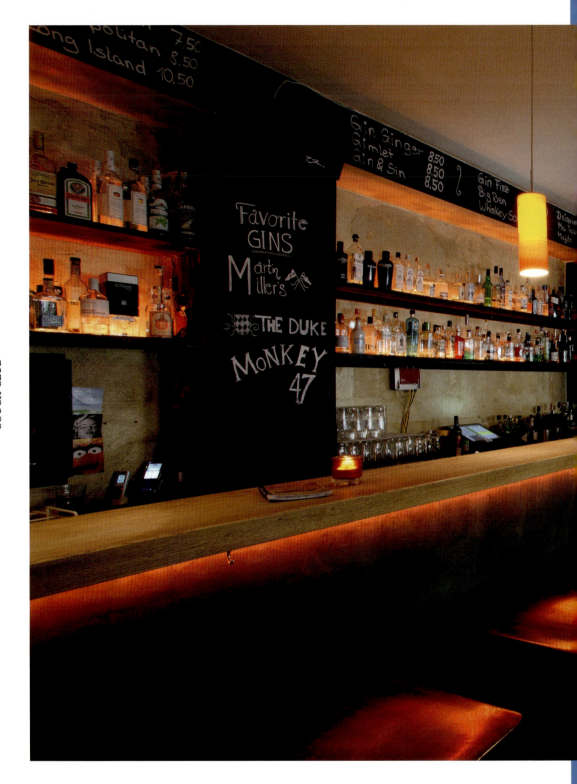

Die Regist-ratur

Damals Club, jetzt Bar; Elektrobeats für Freunde der Nacht; Mehr Drinks als früher; Einfach, stilsicher, ehrlich schlicht und dunkel; Grosse Cocktailauswahl; Mitten im Glockenbachviertel

Club before, now bar; Electro-beats for friends of the night; More drinks than before; Simple, stylish, honestly simple and dark; Great Cocktail selection; In the middle of the Glockenbachviertel

LOCATION Müllerstraße 42, 80469 München • **PHONE** +49 (0)89 203 292 56
WEB www.dieregistratur.de • **MAIL** info@dieregistratur.de

DIE REGISTRATUR

Kilombo

Hier trifft sich nichts Rechtes und nichts Schlechtes; Westendcharme; Mitgebrachtes Essen kein Problem; Abwechslungsreiche Musikauswahl
There is no such thing as right or wrong here; Westen charms; Packed launch is no problem; Varied music collection

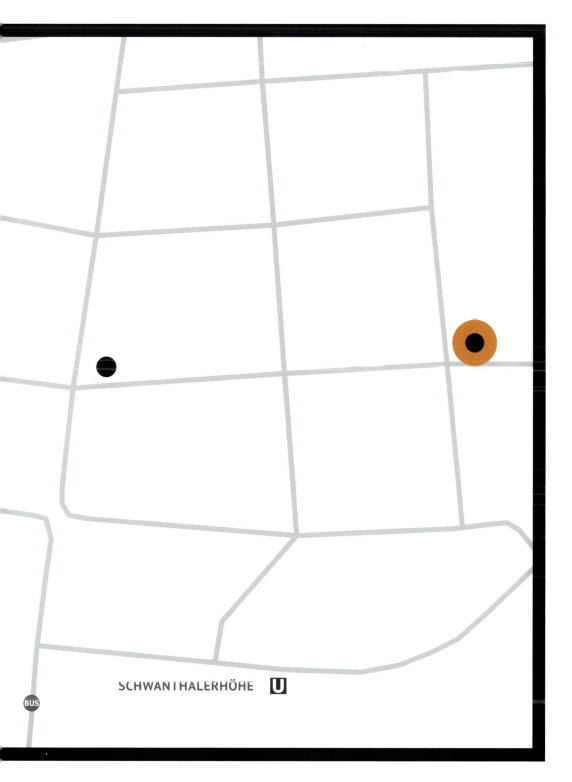

LOCATION Gollierstraße 14A, 80339 München • **PHONE** +49 (0)89 954 55 938
WEB www.kilombom.wordpress.com • **MAIL** email.an.das@kilombo.in

Johannis Café

Bier trinken und plaudern bis spät in die Nacht; Einer der Münchner Klassiker in Haidhausen; Seit mehr als 49 Jahren praktisch unverändert; Matterhorn vor Ort!

Beer drinking and chatting till late at night; One of the Munich classics in Haidhausen; Completely unchanged for more than 49 years; Matterhorn on site!

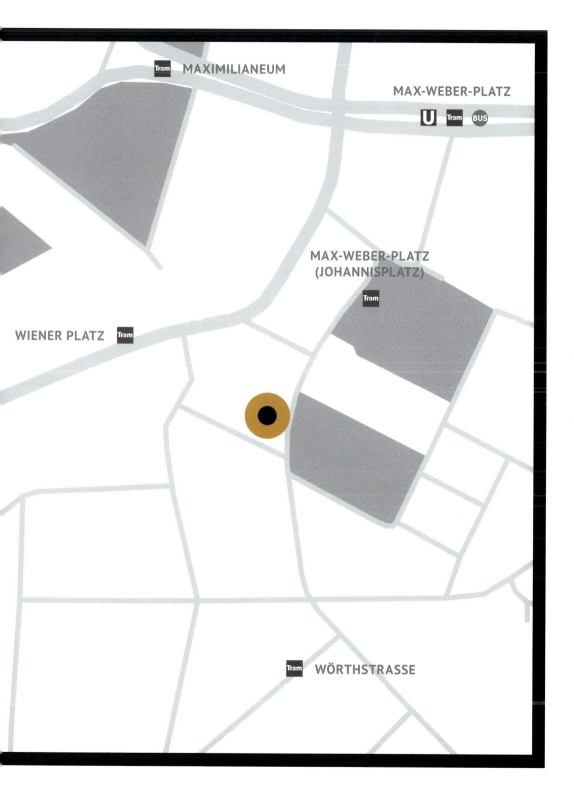

LOCATION Johannisplatz 15, 81667 München • **PHONE** +49 (0)89 48 012 40

JOHANNIS CAFÉ

Café Cord

Ruhig; Ideal, um danach in das Nachtleben zu starten; 50er Jahre Style; Terrasse; Gibt auch Essen; Viele Cocktails; Espressobar bis 3 Uhr morgens geöffnet

Calm; Ideal for starting night life afterwards; 50s Style; Terrace; Also serves food; Many cocktails; Espresso bar open until 3am.

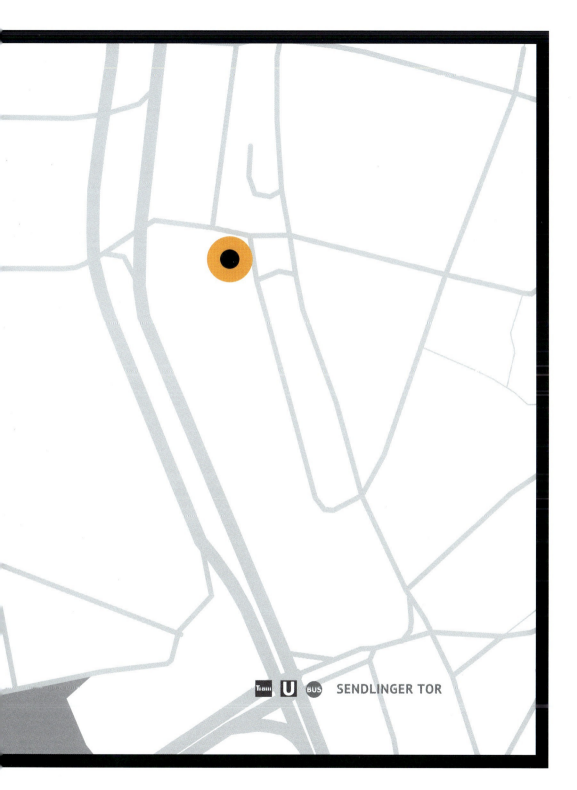

LOCATION Sonnenstraße 19, 80331 München • **PHONE** +49 (0)89 54 540 780
WEB www.cafe-cord.tv • **MAIL** info@cafe-cord.tv

CAFÉ CORD

Stadion

Nach eigenen Angaben die berühmteste Fussballkneipe Deutschlands; Jeder Fan ist willkommen; Gemeinsames Fussballschauen mit reichlich Bier: Ein wunderschönes Vergnügen; Sonntags Tatort schauen und günstige Schnitzel essen; Fussballbibliothek; An der Decke findet man Fussballrasen

According to its own account, it is the most famous soccer pub in Germany; Every fan is welcome; Common football shows with abundant beer; Wonderful pleasure; Watch the German TV classic "Tatort" and eat affordable chips on sundays; Soccer library; You will find football turf on the cielling

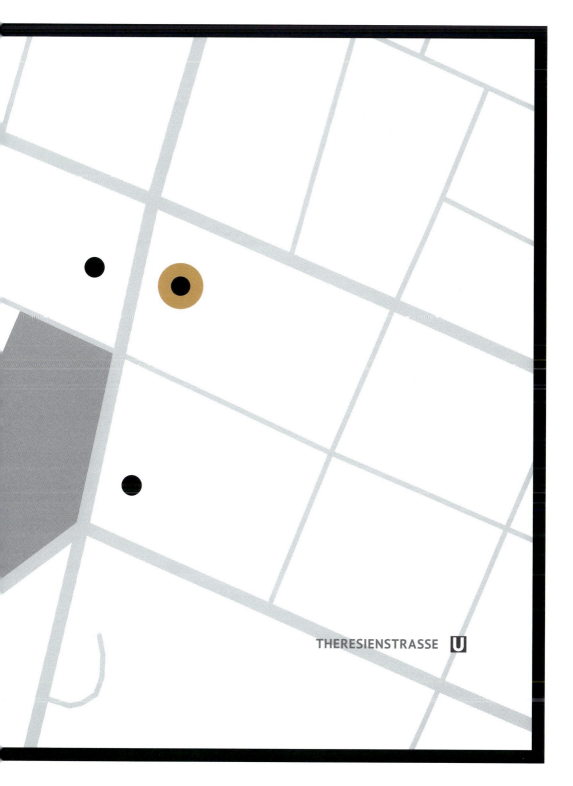

LOCATION Schleißheimer Straße 82, 80797 München • **PHONE** +49 (0)89 529 736
WEB www.stadionanderschleissheimerstrasse.de • **MAIL** info@sadss.de

STADION

Palau

Katalanischer Stil; Spanisch, lässig und entspannt.; Fast wie das Original in Barcelona; Viel Champagner; Wenig Chichi; Man fühlt sich wohl und bekommt nebenbei noch leckere Tapas; Herrlich unprätentiös mit spanischer Musik im Hintergrund; No seats!

Catalan style; Spanish, casual and relaxed.; Almost like the original in Barcelona; Much champagne, little Chichi; One feels at home and at the same time recives tasty tapas; Delightfully unpretentious, with Spanish music in the background; No seats!

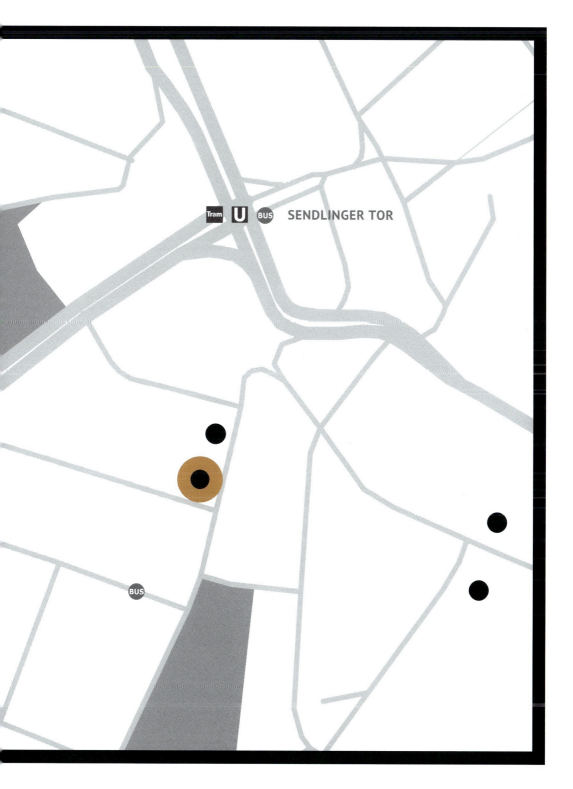

LOCATION Thalkirchner Str. 16, 80337 München • **PHONE** 01525 95 89 137
WEB www.palau-grill.bar • **MAIL** info@palau-grill.bar

PALAU

Bar Comercial

Innenstadtbar mit Verpflegung; Oft sehr voll; Leute kennenlernen leicht gemacht; Schicke Umgebung; Gemischtes Publikum; Sehr geschmackvolle Einrichtung; Umfangreiche Getränkeauswahl

Down town bar with catering; Often very crowded; Knowing people made easy; Nice surroundings; Mixed audience; Very tasteful decor; Extensive collection of drinks

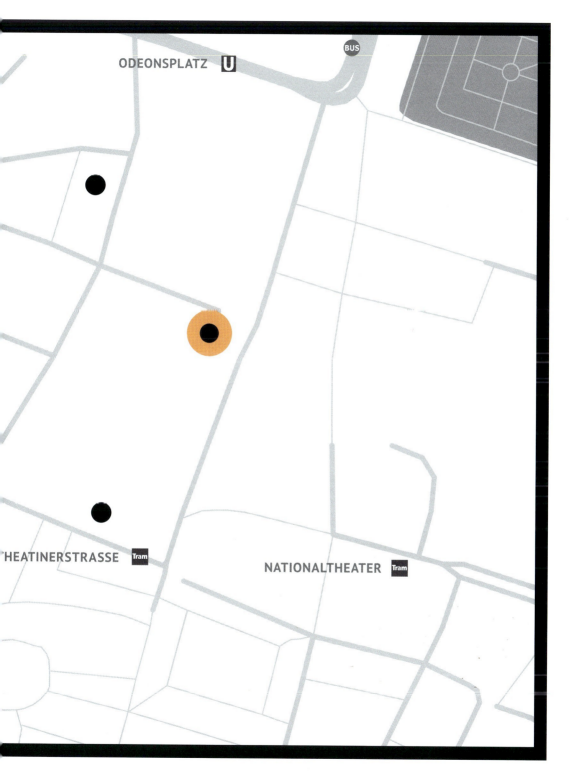

LOCATION Theatinerstraße 16, 80333 München • PHONE +49 (0)89 207 002 66
WEB www.barcomercial.de • MAIL info@barcomercial.de

BAR COMERCIAL

LOLA

Wer das alte Mylord noch kennt, wird sich erinnern: Welch traditionsreicher Ort des Münchner Bar/Nachtlebens; Großer Bartresen; Plüschsofas; Ein für München fast schon anrüchiges Ambiente; Die Geister bereits von uns gegangener Schauspieler und Regisseure wie Hildegard Knef und Rainer Werner Fassbinder scheinen noch immer durch die Räume zu schweben

Whoever still knows the old Mylord will remember: What a traditional place of the Munich bar/nightlife; Large wet bar; Soft sofas; This is an almost amusing atmosphere for Munich; The spirits of actors and directors, such as Hildegard Knef and Rainer Werner Fassbinder, who have already left us, still seem to be hovering through the rooms

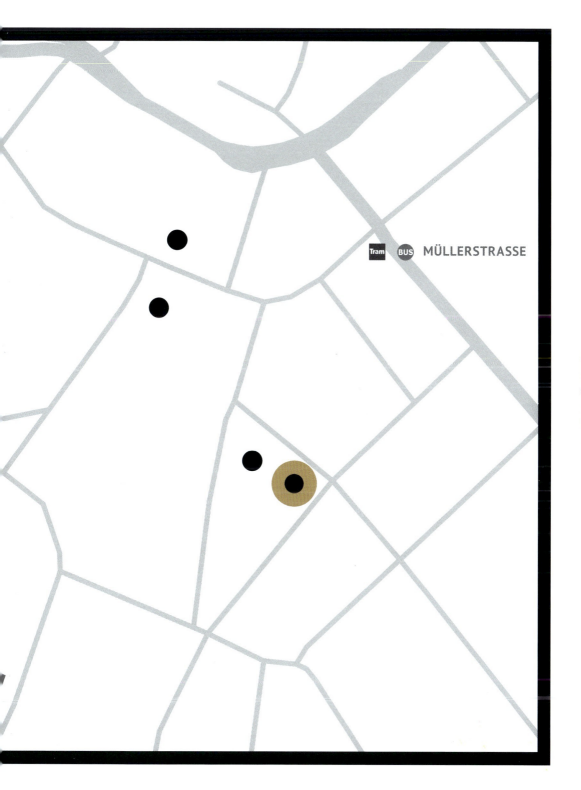

LOCATION Ickstattstraße 2A, 80469 München • **PHONE** +49(0)151 252 469 8
WEB www.lola-bar.de

StammBar

Schottisches München; Eine Bar wie ein Schottlandmuseum; Kilt wird gerne gesehen; Riesiger Fernseher; Viel Edelstahl; Beer Wall direkt aus Irland; Selbstbedienung führt zu viel Kommunikation zwischen den Gästen; Viele Studenten und mehr als 25 Whisky-Sorten bringen eine Menge Spass

Scottish Munich; A bar like a Scotland museum; Kilt is gladly seen; Huge TV; Plenty of stainless steel; Beer Wall directly from Ireland; Self-service leads to much communication between the guests; Many students and more than 25 whiskey varieties bring a lot of fun

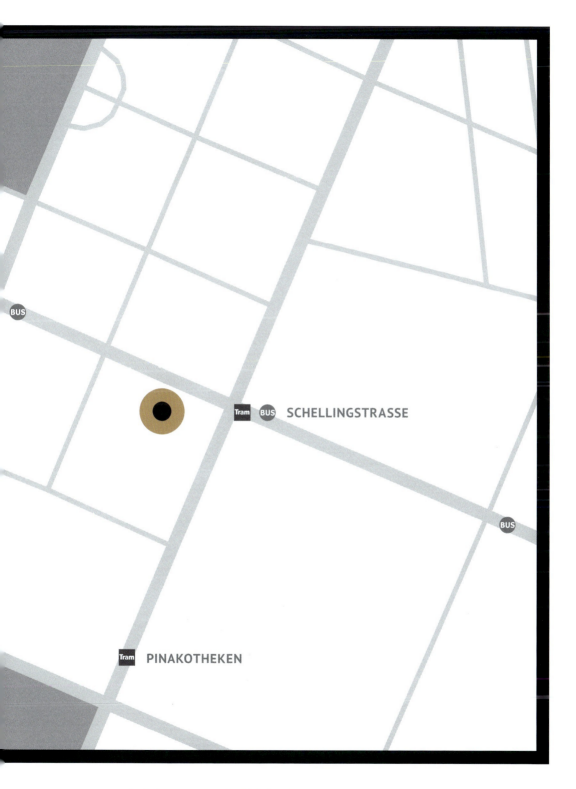

LOCATION Schellingstraße 59, 80799 München • PHONE +49 (0)89 45 227 514
WEB www.stammbar.com • MAIL info@stammbar.com

Blue Spa Lounge & Terrasse

Der Klassiker auf der Terrasse im Hotel Bayerischer Hof; Auch hotelfremde Gäste sind willkommen; Traumhafte Aussicht auf die Stadt bis in die Berge im Süden; Im Winter wird die Terrasse zur Polar-Bar

The classic on the terrace at the Bayerischer Hof Hotel; Foreign hotel guests are also welcome; Fantastic views of the city up into the mountains to the south; In winter, the terrace becomes a polar bar

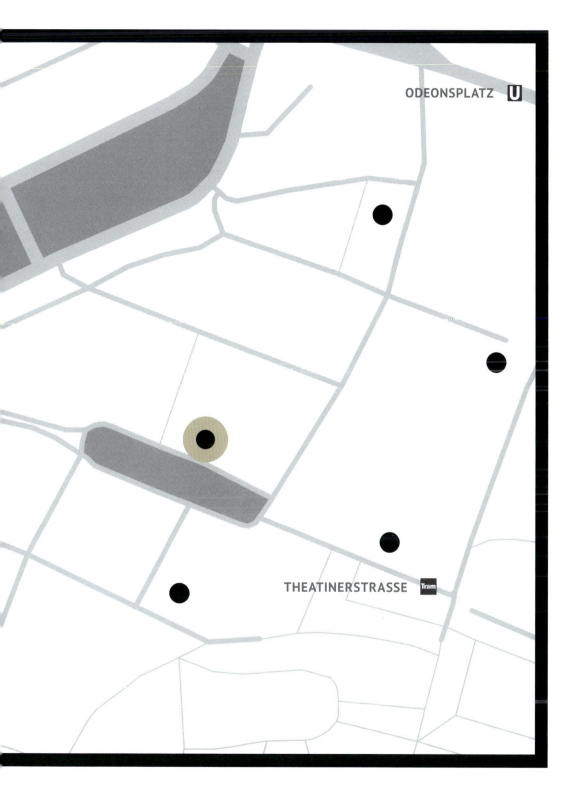

LOCATION Promenadeplatz 6, 80333 München • PHONE +49 (0)89 21 20 875
WEB www.bayerischerhof.de • MAIL bluespa@bayerischerhof.de

Grey's Bar

Hotelbar mit Riesencouch und ausgezeichneten Cocktails, die gerne auch mal flambiert serviert werden; In den Hotelbetrieb H'Otello integriert, daher ein ständiges Kommen und Gehen; Cosmopolites Feeling

Hotel bar with giant couch and excellent cocktails, which are also served sometimes flambéed; Integrated into the H'Otello hotel business, therefore a constant coming and going; Cosmopolite Feeling

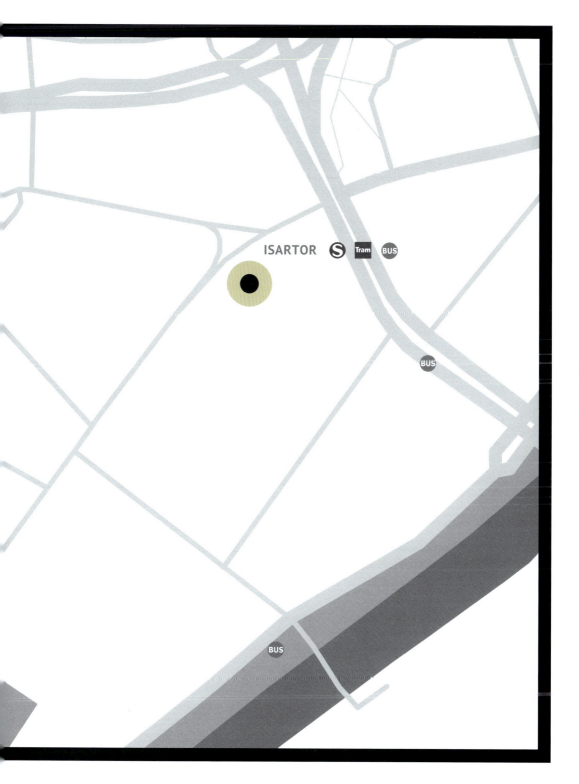

LOCATION Baaderstraße 1, 80469 München • PHONE +49(0)89 21 63 90 01
WEB www.hotello.de • MAIL reservierung@hotello.de

GREY'S BAR

Geyerwally

Bar eines Mieteraktivisten; Ehemalige Boazn im Glockenbachviertel; Kein Techno; Kein Designschick; Ehrlich; Kneipe eben

Bar of activist tenants; Former Boazn in Glockenbach area; No tech; No trendy design; Honest; Just a pub

LOCATION Geyerstraße 17, 80469 München • **PHONE** +49 (0)176 84034005

Bar Gabányi

Wow! So muss eine Bar sein; Braun – beige – schwarz; Ein weiterer Klassiker in München; Mit regelmäßiger Livemusik
Wow! This is how a Bar should be; Brown – beige – black; Another classic in Munich; With regular live music

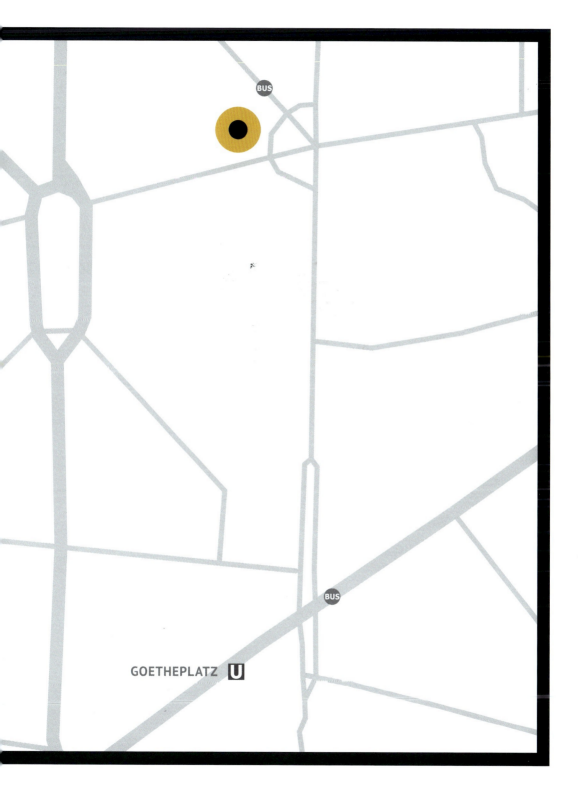

LOCATION Beethovenplatz 2, 80336 München • **PHONE** +49 (0)89 517 018 05
WEB www.bar-gabanyi.de • **MAIL** mail@bar-gabanyi.de

BAR GABÁNYI

Monopol Kino

Programmkino mit Bar; Filme schauen mit Barprogramm; Snacks, Wein und Kinostühle; Auch für Veranstaltungen mit eigenen DVDs buchbar
Cinema with bar; Watch movies with bar program; Snacks, Wine and cinema chairs; Also bookable for events with individual DVDs

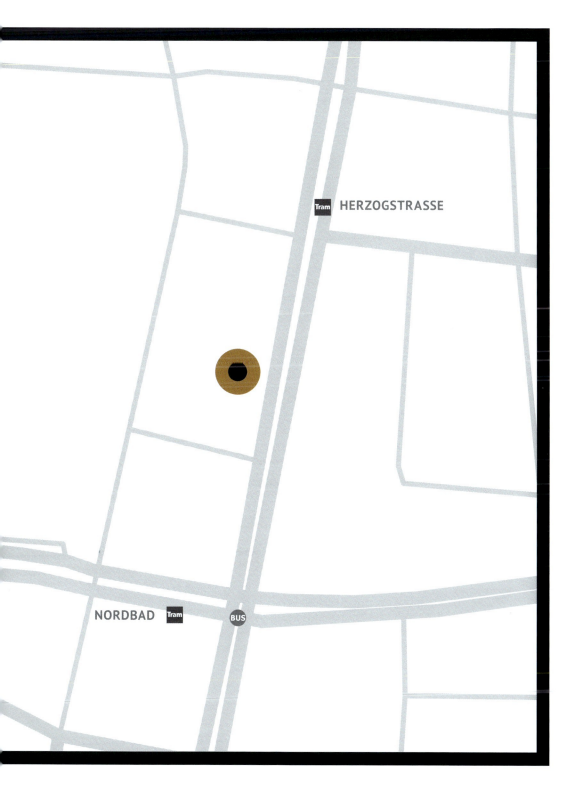

LOCATION Schleißheimer Straße 127, 80797 München • **PHONE** +49 (0)89 38 888 493
WEB www.monopol-kino.de

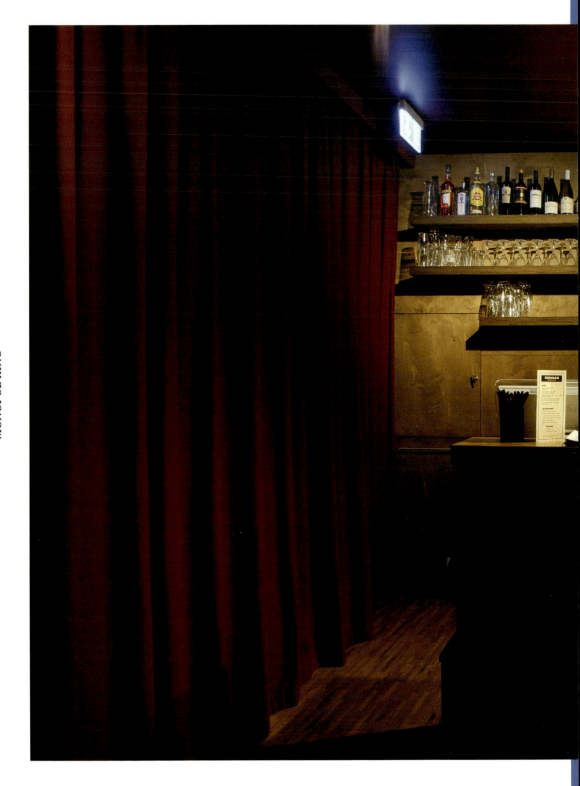

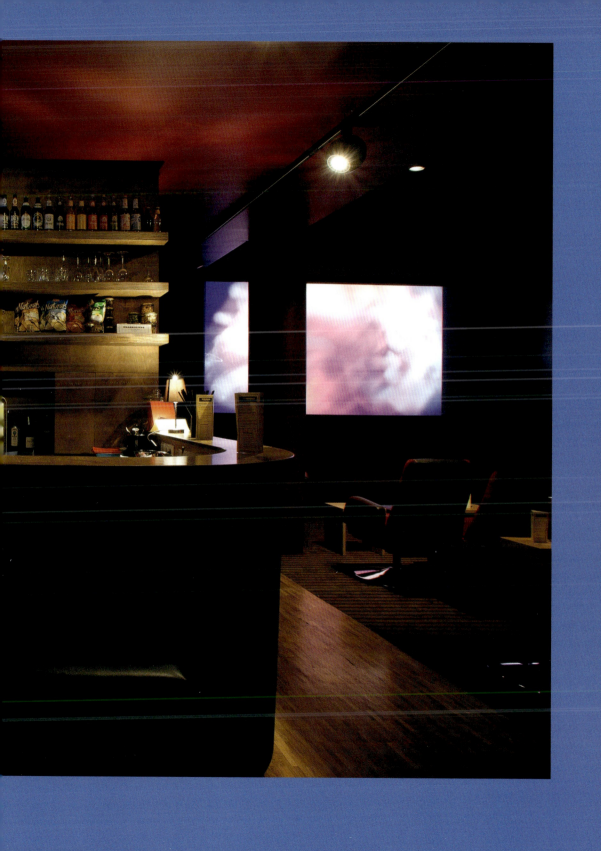

Rational-
theater

Dietmar kümmert sich nicht nur um seine Bargäste, sondern auch um die Kleinkunst in München; Bar mit Bühne und Leinwand für allerhand Künstlerisches; Schwabinger Atmosphäre; Hier treffen sich Anwohner, Trinker und Künstler; So muss eine Bar sein; Sessel, kleine Tische, schummriges Licht; Kultur- und Theaterprogramm; Seit 1965 am Start

Dietmar is not only concerned about his bar guests, but also about the small art in Munich; Bar with stage and screen for all sorts of artistic Schwabinger atmosphere; This is where local people, drinkers and artists meet; This is how a bar should be; Armchairs, small tables, dim light; Cultural and theater program; Since the launch in 1965

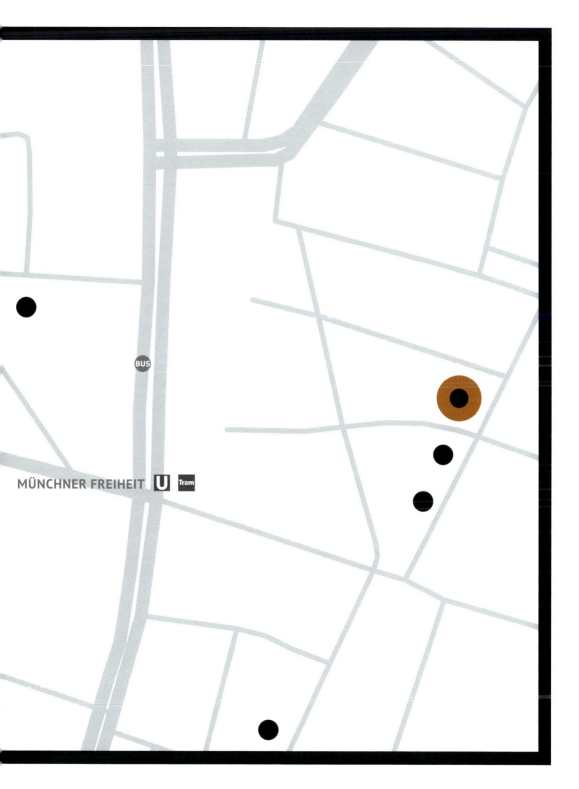

LOCATION Hesseloherstraße 18, 80802 München • **PHONE** +49(0)89 335003
WEB www.rationaltheater.de • **MAIL** mail@rationaltheater.de

RATIONALTHEATER

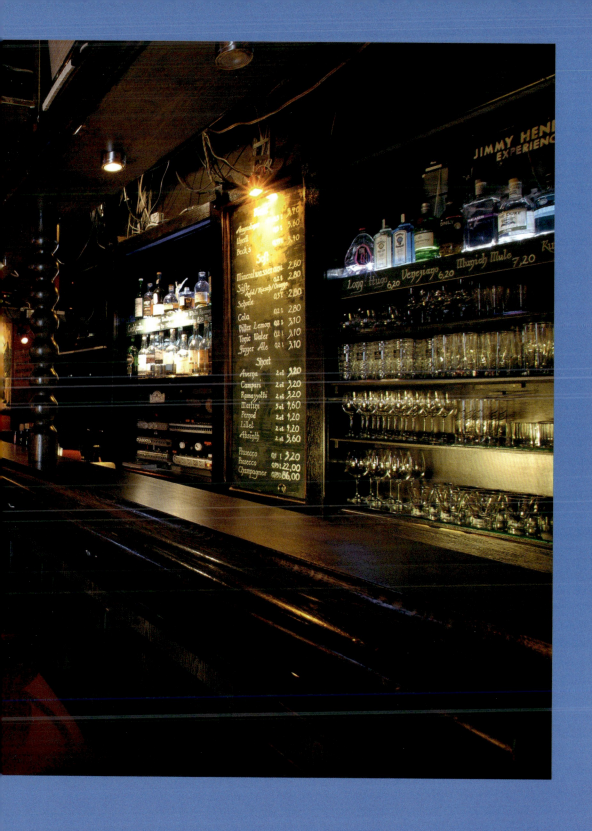

Havana Club

Gemütliche Bar mit James Bond Flair; Hoher Frauenanteil bei den Besuchern; Seit 30 Jahren in München; Ein Klassiker unter den Münchner Bars; Gleich am Isartor; Schön, dass es diese Bar gibt
Cozy bar with James Bond flair; High proportion of female visitors; Since 30 years in Munich; A classic among the Munich bars; Located at the Isartor; A good thing this bar exists

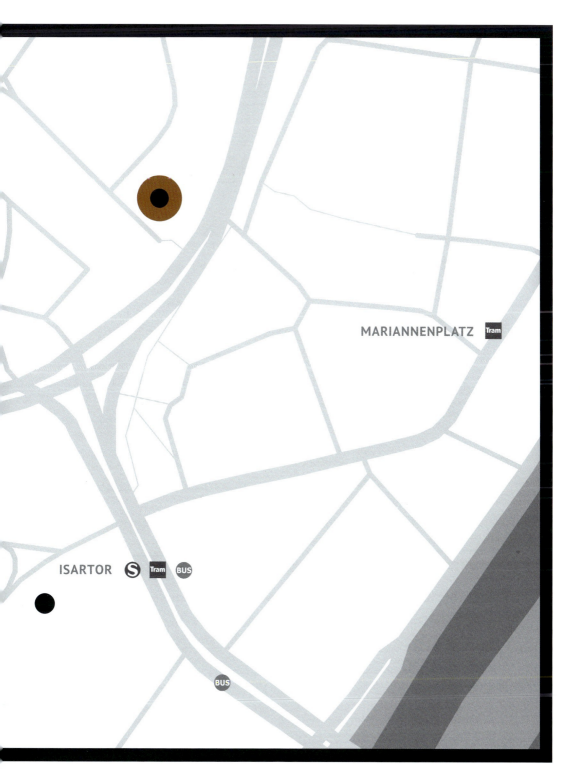

LOCATION Herrnstraße 30, 80539 München • PHONE +49 (0)89 291 884
WEB www.havanaclub-muenchen.de • MAIL info@havanaclub-muenchen.de

Bar Tabacco

Hier hätte sich auch Humphrey Bogart wohlgefühlt; Dunkles Holz; Schwere Sessel; Stilsichere Barleute; Schummriges Licht; Ein Barklassiker in München, der selbst entdeckt werden will; Direkt gegenüber dem Hotel Bayerischer Hof; Der Concierge weiß Bescheid

Humphrey Bogart also felt comfortable here; Dark wood; Heavy armchair; Stable bar people; Dim light; A classic bar in Munich that wants to be discovered; Directly opposite the Bayerischer Hof Hotel; The concierge knows

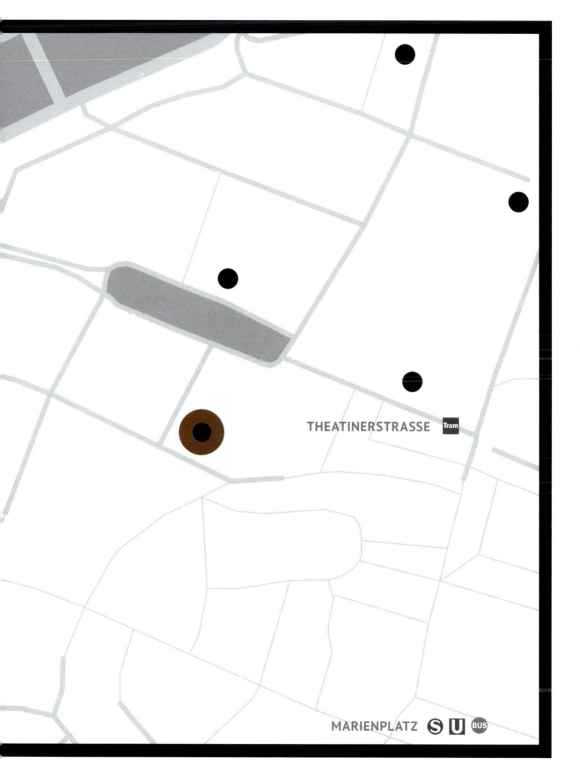

LOCATION Hartmannstraße 8, 80333 München • PHONE +49 (0)89 227 216
WEB www.bartabacco.com

BAR TABACCO

Garçon

Drinks & Thinks; Klassischer Tresen; Unkompliziert; Wunderbare Stimmung; Einfach mal ausprobieren; Gleich beim Viktualienmarkt

Drinks & Thinks; Classic counter; Uncomplicated; Wonderful atmosphere; Just try it out; Located at the Viktualienmarkt

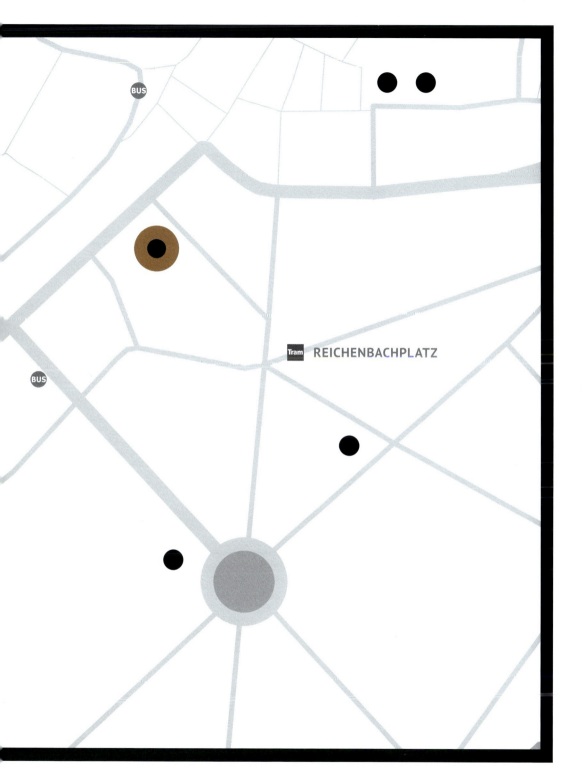

LOCATION Utzschneiderstraße 4, 80469 München
WEB www.bar-garcon.de • MAIL info@bar-garcon.de

GARÇON

The High

Eine Bar, voller Grünpflanzen die dem Namen der Blumenstrasse alle Ehre macht; Super Highballs und eine wirklich grosse Auswahl an Mixgetränken; Hier mischt sich das Münchner Nachtleben; Entspannte Atmosphäre: wenig Sehen und Gesehen werden

A bar full of plants which gives credit to the name Blumenstraße (flower street); Super Highballs and a really large selection of mixed drinks; Munich's nightlife blends here; Atmosphere: see little and avaoid being seen

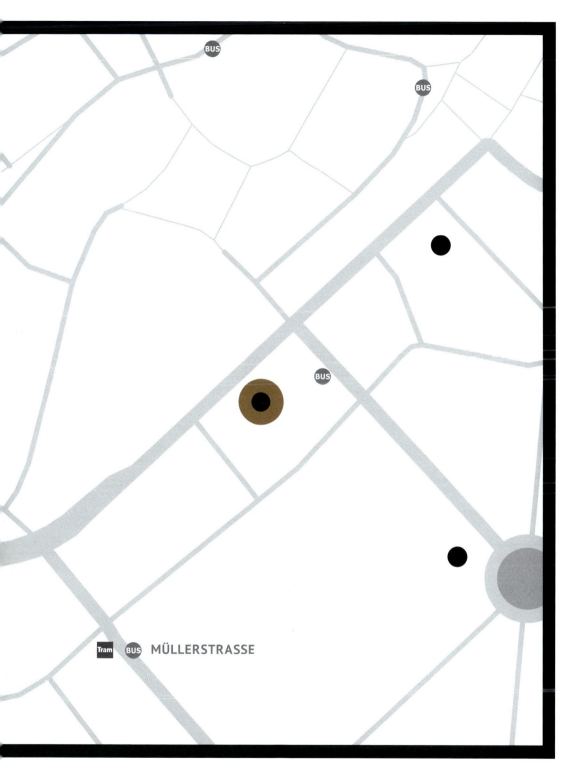

LOCATION Blumenstraße 15, 80331 München • **PHONE** +49 (0)89 089 089
WEB www.drinkourballs.de • **MAIL** info@drinkourballs.com

Mehr!
More!

Was haben Sie mit B|ARS MÜNCHEN erlebt? Erzählen Sie uns davon! — Auf unseren Social Media-Kanälen finden immer wieder spannende Aktionen statt. Besuchen Sie uns doch mal dort.

What experience did you make with B|ARS MUNICH? Tell us about it! — You find us also in social media as you can see below. We are happy to get in touch.

FACEBOOK
www.facebook.com/BarsMonaco

TWITTER
www.twitter.com/istvanju

INSTAGRAM
www.instagram.com/david_de_lourdes

Kontakt:
Contact:

Cocron@icloud.com

Impressum — *Imprint*

B|ARS MÜNCHEN

© 2017 István Cocron

Erste Auflage — *First edition*

Autor, Idee, Text — *Author, Idea, Text:*

ISTVÁN COCRON

Fotografie — *Photography:*

SONJA ALLGAIER

Konzeption, Gestaltung, Satz — *Conception, Design, Typesetting:*

PATRICK HAFNER | IDEENHUNGER MEDIA GMBH

Satz, Illustration — *Typesetting, Illustration:*

ANNIKA GUTEKUNST | IDEENHUNGER MEDIA GMBH

Druck, Weiterverarbeitung — *Production, Processing:*

MEDIENHAUS KASTNER

www.bars-muenchen.net
www.bars-monaco.de

ISBN: 978-3-00-055971-6